2ND EDITION

Mountaintop Experiences

in the Valley

For those who have lived a lifetime in the valley

Effie Darlene Barba

Mountaintop Experiences in the Valley

For those who have lived a lifetime in the valley

2nd Edition

EFFIE DARLENE BARBA

authorHOUSE®

AuthorHouse™
1663 Liberty Drive
Bloomington, IN 47403
www.authorhouse.com
Phone: 1-800-839-8640

First published by AuthorHouse 8/24/2011

ISBN: 978-1-4634-4517-1 (e)
ISBN: 978-1-4634-4516-4 (sc)

Printed in the United States of America

"He told me that during those moments when I lay crumpled in despair from the valley; He, my Savior, prayed for my faith to be strengthened as He never left my side."

Original Artwork by Ronald Barba, my dear son.

Dedication

I have to thank Valentino Elvis who preserved this book in his possession and painstakingly has read it both in its original form and the new edition. His reviews and recommendations have been invaluable to me. Amazingly, God always places the right people in our lives at the right moment to be a blessing to us. My children, Melissa Smith, Alberto Barba, and Ronald Barba have been always and forever foremost in being an inspiration to me. The love and support my children have given me strength. They have been three of God's incredible gifts of Mercy to this humbled child of His. God has step by step transformed my life, my spirit, and my desires as He gently set forth to mold this vessel so He might be Glorified in me. I am grateful for all of the valleys that have led me to seek and savor Him foremost in my life.

Table of Contents

Give Me This Valley

I cried, Lord, please help me climb
This mountain so sublime
Full of health and wealth and fame
Surely there I'd praise your name

But I heard a whispering voice
Said, "for you that's not my choice"
I want you in this valley deep
Where your joy my heart will keep

Lord, you can take that mountain high
And let me stay here by your side
In this valley filled with pain
Where I know you know my name

Give me a life where I might live
Dependent on the Grace you give
I'd rather be here by your side
Than on that great mountainside

Give me the faith and hope that's yours
As your spirit through me pours
To a world in need of you
Give me strength for them to view

Let me show the Glory of Your Hope
Far from that slippery slope
In the valley where you stand
Let me walk and hold your hand

Though the Valley may be dark
You're the light, my precious spark
You are all I need to know
Let me walk now here below

Give me the love of your great smile
That casts aside my selfish guile
Remove my thoughts of selfish pity
Your heart I might see clearly

You are the only one I need
For my soul you have freed
By the valley that you walked
To the cross where you were mocked

So let me walk this valley too
Where there your heart I knew
Keep your mountains filled with pride
Let me stay here at your side.

Introduction

I first completed this book in 2003, proceeded to get the copyright and then sat it aside for all these years. In fact, there were parts of it that I lost when a computer virus hit my computer and destroyed one of the chapters. As I completed another book that lay heavy on my heart, I decided that it was time to start publishing the remainder of my works. Alas, I began the search for the manuscript to no avail. So, I did the only thing I knew to do, ask God to help me find it. Two days later, I got a message on Facebook from someone asking me if I had ever published it because they had proofed it for me back in 2003. I had not kept in touch with this person all these years; yet, they had that day opened a drawer and found the manuscript lying there. Amazing how God works. They promptly mailed me a copy and I tucked it away waiting for the moment that God would provide the money to self publish (I don't propose that as an unknown I would be noticed in the publishing world). You see, only God knows my heart which merely wants to Glorify Him by telling my experiences of His faithfulness throughout my life, even in those moments when I failed Him or for lack of faith plummeted into despair or fear. Last Wednesday (March 2, 2011), I purchased the package to publish these works. I sent the publisher the completed manuscript for "A Broken and Contrite Heart" which I had finished in 2010. I was going to format this book and send it on. Yet, I suddenly realized that as it stands "Mountaintop Experiences in the Valley", in its original 2003 edition does not convey all that it needs to convey in order to be both instructional and comforting to its readers. Perhaps I needed to add some expansions to this book to help guide each of you. Originally I addressed many painful topics beginning with a question and then God's answers in the Bible. I hoped that each of you could be inspired through my struggles, my questions, and God's answers. I want to remind you of the promises of God for each trial of this life. Additionally I want to give you some advice as to how to accomplish and apply each of these promises to your own life. As this is my desire, and after careful prayer I realized I needed to reveal to you more of my life so that you might understand the reason for my turmoil which marks the beginning of each chapter. It is my hope that if I bare my soul honestly I might be able to impact your life and help you through your own trials. I need to be honest as I openly bare much of my life to you. My attempt will be to leave the original chapters with as few of changes as possible because they display the raw emotion of where I stood before God at that exact moment in time. I do believe God is leading me to additionally include both an introduction and post discussion for each chapter. The introduction will tell you about those events in my life that lead to that chapter and will be titled the prelude. The post discussion will be the description of how to apply God's promises to your own life and will be called therefore. Thus reflecting that because of everything that was just said, therefore the steps we need to take are laid out for us. I pray that God guide my hand because my fear is to create a fragmentation by applying three styles of writing in one book. God is the only one who knows how to do just that so well in His Word, the Bible by using prose, poetry, history, and parables to express His love and instruction for us. I can tell you that every step of this journey with God has been a part of His transforming work in me. Every moment of my life including those moments of my own failures, the moments of deep pain and sorrow, the moments of triumph have worked together to draw me closer to Him. He has revealed Himself to me through each miniscule detail of my life tempered with great preachers, His word, Great Hymns, and hours of prayer. The more He revealed Himself, the greater my desire became to know Him even more. The greater my desire to know Him, the greater peace, hope, and joy I have experienced in my life. The greater my hope and joy the more my heart erupted in praise, which then again drew me ever closer to Him. He knows that He is the only One who can fill that empty void within each person born, because sin has separated us from the one true purpose of mankind—which is to Glorify God and by such be Glorified to reflect back Glory to God. Even when I did not understand His Plan it was perfect, as only He could know what it would take to change this human heart into one that could see and savor Christ. He saw the depth of my heart and knew exactly what chaff needed to be removed to clear my vision of Christ. He knew that there are heights of joy and peace that can only be found when we see Christ in all His Glory. Therefore, He also knew that many times the Mountaintop Experiences can only be found in the Valley of Despair. It was in those valleys where I became completely stripped of myself and driven to the foot of the cross so that Christ could perform a great exchange. He takes my fears, my despair, my sin and my guilt and gives me His hope, His joy, His righteousness and His Glory so that I might reflect that same Glory back to Him for a dying world to see. It has seemed sometimes in my limited mind a tedious road; yet, actually, God has been so patiently drawing me ever closer to Him. As I look around me, I realize that many of my circumstances have not changed so much; but I have changed and the trials now appear as opportunities rather than crosses to bear. Joy is found in Him, in the words of a song of praise to Him who has been faithful to love me each step of the way. I have learned two very important truths during my life. One is that my entire lifetime is but a brief moment compared to eternity. The other, no pain is too great to bear if it leads to the salvation of one soul. There have been many moments when I felt so unworthy of God's love, still He never let go of me. In the magnificence of this His Universe, I am so unimportant—a mere grain of sand; yet, to Him I am utterly important. What an amazing truth that is.

Prelude to From Valley to Valley
—pain and illness

When I wrote the chapter from Valley to Valley, I had just been told that they had found a mass in the head of my pancreas. As a nurse practitioner and with a history of cancer, my first thought was that this mass could mean I had pancreatic cancer. I was well aware that pancreatic cancer had only few survivors. In addition, I knew that it was an excruciatingly painful disease. As a widow with my children in college or married, I felt very alone during that time. Besides, I did not want to worry my children with the thought that I now might have pancreatic cancer. They had been through too many trials in their young lives already. I wanted them to have a chance to enjoy their youth before they would have to face another parent's death. At that time in my life I was very weary of the journey. I had no fear if God chose to take me home. Yet, I could not imagine my children going through the trauma of worrying about my health or possible death. For that reason I had to shield them from my being sick as long as I could. They had already seen me going through chemo only a few years earlier while they were still in high school. My husband and their father had died tragically in 1994. Though a brilliant surgeon, he had suffered from a bipolar disorder which had led to many difficulties in their own lives. Yet, that is a different story. In 1997, I decided to get my Master's Degree in Nursing. So with the permission of my children I began the two years of commuting from Dexter, MO to Nashville, TN. I left on Sunday night and returned on Friday evening. Despite my calling my sons every day from the dorm, I missed out on a lot of their high school events. Yet, I continued because I believed that my furthering my education would ultimately be for the good of the family. In December 1998, I was diagnosed with a very aggressive form of breast cancer. So I had undergone a mastectomy with tram-flap reconstruction which was followed by chemotherapy. I was in a trial study and the drugs I received were toxic to the neurological system as well. Anyone who has undergone chemotherapy could appreciate how tough chemotherapy can be. I pressed forward through school because I knew that if I quit, I would not return. Beyond that if I stopped school my school loans would be placed immediately into repayment mode. Money was tight as it was with my not being able to work during the chemotherapy (The hospitals refused to allow a neutropenic nurse around patients.) There was no money to pay the school loans. Besides, I had two sons which I needed to somehow get through college. Three to four months after completing the chemo, I was diagnosed with ulcerative colitis. My ulcerative colitis remained in constant flare despite diet, massive steroids, and medications for over a year. There was no choice at that time but to have my colon removed and have a pouch reconstruction. By the time I underwent surgery in late 2000, I had already developed the severe side effects of the steroids. I was very cushinoid, including the fact that I had a full beard and mustache. My large muscles were so weak I had to pull myself up the stairs holding tightly to the rails so as not to fall. Despite the severity of my illness, I was able to continue working to try to support myself and my sons. This I did more by God's strength than by my own. Following the surgery the steroids were stopped, so then I had overwhelmingly severe fatigue which I had to fight against. It took all of 2001 to begin to recover from the steroids and get accustomed to my new intestinal system. Then about March 2002, I was told that I had a mass on the head of the pancreas which needed further workup to determine whether it was cancer or not. That was when I wrote From Valley to Valley. For those of you going through illness, I have blogged about the illness in greater detail on my website http://www.mygclorytoglory.com. In the website blogs, I describe all the pain and the sorrow and the suffering that I felt during those years. By 2002 I was extremely wearied from the journey and I needed to know that God had a plan.

From Valley to Valley

"*28 Hast thou not known? hast thou not heard, that the everlasting God, the LORD, the Creator of the ends of the earth, fainteth not, neither is weary? there is no searching of his understanding. 29 He giveth power to the faint; and to them that have no might he increaseth strength. 30 Even the youths shall faint and be weary, and the young men shall utterly fall: 31 But they that wait upon the LORD shall renew their strength; they shall mount up with wings as eagles; they shall run, and not be weary; and they shall walk, and not faint.*" Isaiah 40: 28-31

So often I have stood before the Lord and wished that I could just see God's plan. Surely the pain and suffering that I am enduring has a purpose in His plan? Is this all punishment for my sin, my failure to be able to live up to the law? Yet, my salvation is by Grace and not of my own works; so how could that be the case? I have sought Him all these years and have only wanted to please Him; despite which I have often failed in this walk. Does His love and His Promises depend on my getting it right? Must I remain forever living in the valleys until somehow I pull myself up and force myself to become a better person and prove to God I am worthy of His love? Otherwise, will I remain forever in this valley, a hopeless failure as His child? Or is there something more that I am to gain from this valley and it has nothing to do with punishment; but, rather an opportunity to grow? Does this pain and suffering have a purpose as it did in the lives of David, Daniel, Peter, John, and Paul? If that is the case would it not be easier to tolerate or go through if only

He would reveal to me His purpose and His plan? Yet, if I knew the end; would it still require faith to go through it? Hebrews 11:1 "Now **faith** is the substance of things hoped for, the **evidence** of things **not seen**." Those are questions that have pressed within my mind so often in my lifetime that I dare not try to number them all. There had been so many valleys in my life with little reprieve that I suddenly believed that I would spend my lifetime only in valleys of pain, sorrow and suffering. I trudged forward so many times believing that if I could only remain faithful, I would be rewarded with reaching the mountaintop where I could then rest and enjoy the remainder of my life basking in His Glory with no further problems. Perhaps a part of my human nature wanted to believe the prosperity gospel. Somehow I believed that if I just held on and made myself have a little more faith I would be blessed with earthly riches, companionship, and even fame for my faithfulness. Foolish thinking, I guess, but it was what I strove for. Like Job had everything restored, I believed that if I worked hard enough to please God through the trials then I would be blessed as well. I was then shocked as each time I thought I had championed a trial, it was either quickly followed by an even greater trial or my utter failure toward God. Sometimes I just thought that if I tried a little harder, then God would really love me. I believed that if I could spiritually grow enough, then the world's ideas of prosperity would be mine. It is comical that I could have even believed such a lie. A review of the scripture would reveal the fact that many times God's appointed suffered greatly for the sake of Christ. Look at the lives of the apostles who did not experience prosperity as they went about faithfully proclaiming the name of Christ. If worldly prosperity had not been the rewards for faithfulness for the apostles, then, I had no basis to proclaim this as a promise for myself either.

Shouldn't the experience of my former trials have helped me to understand the truth about suffering in the life of the believer? So many times I had stood at this point of fearfulness and questioning in my life only to later find myself marveling at His majesty and His Grace that lead me through the valley. All the trials, failures, and sorrows of my past God had taken and molded into beautiful blessings. Knowing this, I should be able to wait patiently for Him to reveal His plan. Still I found myself tremulous at the thought of this valley of uncertainty that lay before me. My human nature wanted to run ahead of Him to try to work it all out. I wished so to run ahead to the top of the mountain and just skip the valley that lay before me. Surely my testimony and praise would be greater from the mountaintop where the entire world could hear my voice. I have many times reminded God that I am really not good at this thing called pain. In fact, didn't He remember how much grumbling or crying I had done at times in the past? Surely, my testimony of a loving God would be tainted by this valley approach He proposed. I reminded Him that I was too fragile and too weary to be able to do this. How could a faltering and stumbling child bring Him Glory? Instead He led me to the edge of the precipice and bid me leap into the darkness below (metaphorically, I really don't want anyone jumping physically off of cliffs). Patiently and gently He bid me to trust Him. As my eyes had pierced through the dark, snarly valley below me I had seen there in the midst of the darkness suddenly a light illuminating a small section and Christ stood there. He bid me to come and follow Him. He had then reminded me of all the valleys we had already passed through. He reminded me of how near to me He had stood during those times and how much He had taught me of His Grace and His Love. He reminded me of how much He had revealed to me of His love, His omnipotence, His faithfulness, and His omniscience during those dark valleys of my past. He told me that during those moments when I lay crumpled in despair from the valley; He, my Savior, prayed for my faith to be strengthened as He never left my side.

So, here it was that once more I had found that I was facing a future ahead of such deep uncertainty. It would appear that the road was dimmed by such darkness that the mere thought of facing into that precipice caused me to shutter in despair. The darkness and its cold chill wrapped around my body and caused me cry out, "Please God remove this pain and torment because I cannot bear it. Or if you choose not to remove it, please at least show me what purpose you have for me in this trial. Dear Lord, show me the end, that I might understand the journey." Yet, the only answer I heard was "Trust me." Trust can be so difficult when you see the potential of chronically living in pain or suffering. It is very difficult when it would appear that all your former hopes and dreams have been shattered and you are left with emptiness. Trust seems only to be a word when everything inside feels as though you are falling apart. Yet, as I gazed into this dark valley, I was once more reminded of how often I have stood there before. Each trial had been quite different; yet each seemed so impossible at the time I had faced them. Still, it was God who walked me through each trial and each had brought me closer to Him while revealing more of Himself each and every time.

When God's answer is "trust me", my response should be to let go of my feelings and rely solely on the truth of who God is and to rest assured in knowing the Heart of God as He has revealed it to me in times past. It is only by doing this that I might have the ability to "wait upon Him and mount up with wings as an eagle." If I had never walked through a trial before would I know Him well enough to be able to face a new trial? Whenever a storm came while the apostles were in the boat they became frightened. Not just once or even twice, but three times. Jesus very patiently taught them each time that He was sufficient for the storm. This was a lesson that they needed to learn before His crucifixion and resurrection because they would be facing even greater storms as they began to spread the gospel to the very world that had crucified Christ.

I shared another human frailty with the apostles. That was looking around me to the lives of other Christians positions with jealously. Why was it that some seemed to live always on the mountaintop? Some looked at me with my trials and said, "You must have done something to anger God." Or "Maybe you weren't ever saved." Others seemed to have found this Christian life so easy, demonstrating such amazing faith from the beginning. Others appeared to have their lives filled with what appeared to be prosperity. I need a reminder when I envy these; that God works out His wonders differently with each child. Sometimes the children whom He calls to great service, must be molded, sifted, and purified that they might serve Him. They need to be stripped of all that would draw them away, so He might be all that they can see or rely on. In John 21 it is recorded about Simon Peter as God revealed to him of his future of a painful death. *"¹⁸Verily, verily, I say unto thee, When thou wast young, thou girdest thyself, and walkedst whither thou wouldest: but when thou shalt be old, thou shalt stretch forth thy hands, and another shall gird thee, and carry thee whither thou wouldest not. ¹⁹This spake he, signifying by what death he should glorify God. And when he had spoken this, he saith unto him, Follow me. ²⁰Then Peter, turning about, seeth the disciple whom Jesus loved following; which also leaned on his breast at supper, and said, Lord, which is he that betrayeth thee? ²¹Peter seeing him saith to Jesus, Lord, and what shall this man do? ²²Jesus saith unto him, If I will that he tarry till I come, what is that to thee? follow thou me."*

If you have ever passed through a dark valley or are facing one now, I bid you walk through this journey with me. My lifetime has been in the dark valleys and I have learned in those valleys just how marvelous His Grace truly is. I have learned the true meaning of Isaiah 40:31 *"They that wait upon the Lord shall mount up with wings as Eagles, they shall run and not grow weary, they shall walk and not faint"*

To grasp the true meaning of this verse, one must understand how eagles fly. They spread their wings forth with hardly any effort and with the winds to carry them they soar or float to their destination usually landing deep in a valley. Their flight is effortless, as they trust on the wind currents to hold them suspended in the air and carry them downward to their destination with great precision. God's promise is that when we reach forth without any self effort to leap into the unknown future He calls us to, He will be that wind current which guides us precisely to the destination He has planned in love. Even though it may look dark and uninviting to us, He has always the best plan to bring us His Hope and Joy.

I know that He is a God of love who reaches out with the loving arms of a Father to protect and guide His children. He has proven that in His Love letters to us. John 3:"*¹⁶For God so loved the world that he gave his only begotten Son, that whosoever believeth in him should not perish, but have everlasting life.*" **Romans 8: "** *³²He that spared not his own Son, but delivered him up for us all, how shall he not with him also freely give us all things?*" **Jeremiah 29: "**"*¹¹For I know the thoughts that I think toward you, saith the LORD, thoughts of peace, and not of evil, to give you an expected end. ¹²Then shall ye call upon me, and ye shall go and pray unto me, and I will hearken unto you.*" **John 14:**"*¹⁶And I will pray the Father, and he shall give you another Comforter, that he may abide with you forever; ¹⁷Even the Spirit of truth; whom the world cannot receive, because it seeth him not, neither knoweth him: but ye know him; for he dwelleth with you, and shall be in you. ¹⁸I will not leave you comfortless: I will come to you. ¹⁹Yet a little while, and the world seeth me no more; but ye see me: because I live, ye shall live also. ²⁰At that day ye shall know that I am in my Father, and ye in me, and I in you. ²¹He that hath my commandments, and keepeth them, he it is that loveth me: and he that loveth me shall be loved of my Father, and I will love him, and will manifest myself to him. ...²⁵These things have I spoken unto you, being yet present with you. ²⁶But the Comforter, which is the Holy Ghost, whom the Father will send in my name, he shall teach you all things, and bring all things to your remembrance, whatsoever I have said unto you. ²⁷Peace I leave with you, my peace I give unto you: not as the world giveth, give I unto you. Let not your heart be troubled, neither let it be afraid.*" **Joshua 1:9** "*Have not I commanded thee? Be strong and of a good courage; be not afraid, neither be thou dismayed: for the LORD thy God is with thee whithersoever thou goest.*"

All of these promises, I must cling to when facing a valley. You see, when I am near that mountaintop and God calls me back into the dark and unknown valley, a part of me cries out-"please let me touch this mountaintop first" Can I rest there for a little while? After climbing so far with the peak in site, "Surely God, there is where you want me to go?" I try to remind Him that I am too weary and too weak; surely I will mess things up in the valley. "How can I tell people of God's perfect Love while trudging through a deep valley of pain?" "Maybe, Lord, you need someone just a little more noble and who has a lot more of their own faith?" Then to my protests He gently responds once more, "Trust me". His gentle voice bids me leap into the darkness. He reminds me once more of His faithfulness and that His thoughts are higher than I could ever imagine. He assures me that His presence will be with me in the valley. He reminds me of all my journeys through pain and His magnificent Grace that carried me through.

Despite my fear and hesitation, I know that His heart of love would only ask I face the valley if it would bring good to either me or someone else in His kingdom. His promise in Romans 8 *"²⁸And we know that all things work together for good to them that love God, to them who are the called according to his purpose. ²⁹For whom he did foreknow, he also did predestinate to be conformed to the image of his Son, that he might be the firstborn among many brethren. ³⁰Moreover whom he did predestinate, them he also called: and whom he called, them he also justified: and whom he justified, them he also glorified."* His promise is not that all things in and of themselves are good; but rather that they all work together for our good. His goal is that I might be "conformed to the image of his Son" Only an omniscient, omnipotent God could know what needs to occur that I might look like Jesus one day. That transformation I am certain will take a lifetime in my case. So, knowing all this and remembering how gently he has taught me and drawn me to trust Him through the dark storms and valleys of my life; I must join David in saying *"Yea, though I walk through the valley of the shadow of death, I will fear no evil; for thou art with me."* Psalm 23:4

It is for that reason that truly today I will reach forth my wings and gladly fall forward into the unknown valley. Trusting my Heavenly Father, I am amazed at how easy it is now to turn my back on that mountaintop and lunge forth in the valley below wherever it may lead. Has He given me that faith or has it been the lifetime of valleys that taught me to trust His Heart? I have truly learned that He is sufficient for all and as Paul the Apostle cried out "I *have learned, in whatsoever state I am, therewith to be content*" Philippians 4:11. He is truly marvelous and awesome and worthy of our praise not merely on the mountaintops but deep inside the darkest valleys.

What is your valley today? Does it feel as though it is closing in around you? I intrigue you to follow me as I step forth into this valley without fear because of all that He has taught me, all that He has been and all that He is. You see, if He chooses to take me home, I am ready to go. If it is a heavy cross I must bear, I know He will be there to carry it with me. If merely I am to learn from the journey, I pray that He open my heart and mind to receive what He has for me to learn. Or, perhaps, my facing this valley and being forced to recall all the painful valleys I have traveled and fears I have confronted in the past may be so that I may help someone else in the Kingdom of God. Maybe all of this has been just for you. Whatever the reason, God knows, so I will step forth into this darkness and this unknown with great joy. I pray that He holds my wings steady so that I might be a blessing to someone and that I might graciously fulfill His desire. Yet, I know that this is not in my own strength. Instead I want to let go and let Him work in me whatever miracle He has in store for my life. My prayer is that He guides me through the telling of His wonder, for truly, I know that I am too fragile for this endeavor alone. This book, I write to praise Him for He is worthy of our praise. Much like Paul I am reminded in Corinthians 1: "*26For ye see your calling, brethren, how that not many wise men after the flesh, not many mighty, not many noble, are called: 27But God hath chosen the foolish things of the world to confound the wise; and God hath chosen the weak things of the world to confound the things which are mighty; 28And base things of the world, and things which are despised, hath God chosen, yea, and things which are not, to bring to nought things that are: 29That no flesh should glory in his presence. 30But of him are ye in Christ Jesus, who of God is made unto us wisdom, and righteousness, and* sanctification, and redemption: [31]*That, according as it is written, He that glorieth, let him glory in the Lord."*

If by revealing my weakness, I point you toward Christ; then it is worth it all. If the valleys of my life brings one person to Christ and changes their eternity; then it has been worth every tear that I have cried.

My dear Heavenly Father, thank you for all that you have shown me in the darkest valleys. Thank you for allowing me to soar. Help those who struggle with the pain and sorrows of this life, bring forth thy joy and peace in their hearts. Teach them to soar above their pain. In the precious name of Jesus I pray, Amen.

Therefore From Valley to Valley

So how do we get rid of the fear and tremors when we are facing tough valleys in our lives? How do we find joy, hope, peace and mountaintop experiences while in the valley? The steps I am about to outline are meant for those who know Jesus Christ as the Savior; if you don't I urge to ask Him into your heart. He took your sins upon Himself and died on the cross so that you might have the chance to be justified. (Declared just as if you had never sinned) Thereby, you are given the opportunity of a personal, intimate relationship with God. Additionally, by accepting Christ, you become the recipient of all of His promises. This, I declare to you is the key to a life abundantly filled with joy no matter what storm surrounds you.

Now I will get back to the steps to take as a Christian when facing a sudden dark valley.

1. Pray. There is power in prayer. Even if you do not know what to say, just sit quietly before God. The Holy Spirit will make intercession for you. Pray even if you are feeling frustrated or angry with God; because He knows already how you are feeling. This prayer is not because God doesn't know; but it gives Him a moment alone with Him so He can soothe and comfort you.

2. If there is ever a time that you need to be studying your Bible morning and evening or sometimes all day long, it is when facing a valley. It is better to study the Bible everyday, but especially during the valleys you need to increase your time in

the word. How can you claim His promises, if you don't know what they are?

3. Remember every trial (big or small) you have ever been through in the past and remember how God had carried you through. I even suggest writing them down. Trial and across from it the miracle or good change that came about in your heart as a result of the trial. If you have never done this, it may take a moment to reflect backwards and see what good came of each sorrowful moment. Ask God for the wisdom to reveal this to you. You will be amazed at the Grace and Mercy that was etched in the center of that painful trial.

4. Make a list of God's promises concerning finances, illness, loss or whatever your valley is. Keep those scriptures with you and reread them frequently

5. Find Christian Songs that declare His Might and Power and Love—hum them to your own self throughout the day.

6. Each morning make a list of those things for which you are thankful to God and read them to God.

7. Do not skip meals or do without sleep. Even if you don't want to eat, do it anyway. If you awaken in the night, pray quietly while taking deep slow breathes—you can hear God's response clearer when you quiet your own mind. Let yourself drift back to sleep. This is not your moment to diet or deprive yourself of sleep.

8. Neither should you spend all day in bed. Get up and put one foot in front of the other, one step at a time until you do finish that day something you can call an accomplishment—then say "Thank you, Lord for today.

All of these steps I have learned over the years after passing through many trials. True faith, hope, and trust come from seeing God's faithfulness through the trials. Having seen this fact played out in my own life, should I not now see each trial as a gift of love from God? God so carefully and patiently has been working to remove all my own false securities that I might find security in the only one who keeps me safe in the storms of life. He has ever so gently changed my desires that they might be conformed to His desires. How well He has known me. He knew that I, perhaps like Peter, desired to rely on my own strength or to think too much of myself at times. There have been times when He would allow me to press forward in my own strength only to fail and plummet into self despair before looking up and finding my comfort once more in Him, the only strength or righteousness which could be mine. My boss once told me that he did not understand me because whenever God threw me a curveball, I seemed to catch it and run with it as though a great gift. I told Him that had not always been the case; rather, I have learned through many trials that He is faithful and that He loves me beyond anything I could imagine. It is for that reason I can now trust Him. Perhaps that is why last year as I went in for a major surgery, I had no fear. It proved to be one for which the recovery was more painful than I could have imagined; yet, I saw it through God's eyes this time. The pain limited my activity, so I finished writing "A Broken and Contrite Heart." It was a book God had pressed on my heart to write ever since 2005; yet, steadily and slowly He had taught me, sifted me so that I would be ready to write the book. Then, He sat me down for a period of time so that I could do just that. I have learned that when life does not make sense; trust in He who rules the Universe because He is still in control and has a plan of love for me.

This is what happened to Abraham over the years. He at moments had shown great faith, moments of fear, and at moments had tried to help God fulfill His promises. Yet, this all culminated in that great moment of faith when he took Isaac at God's command to the land of Moriah to sacrifice him as a burnt offering. This was his beloved son, the heir of promise whom he had waited a lifetime to be born; yet, with great faith that God had a plan, He marched forth to carry out the command. Abraham had not always shown such faith; yet, through trials and sorrows, he had learned to trust God—no matter what the cost appeared to be. I urge you to go back and read the life of Abraham for more insight into the life of this patriarch of the faith.

So, when life makes no sense; trust God for who He is. He is in control of every detail of your life. Not a hair of your head falls, but He knows and ordains it. His plan is to bring you to a place of hope, joy, faith, and glory as only can be found in an intimate relationship with Him.

Prelude to Whiter Than Snow
(Dealing with Guilt)

Of all the preludes for this book, I feel this is the most difficult one to write. For me to tell you of how I felt and why, it is important that I reveal some failures which I pray will not hurt those around me. Even though I believe we should never be afraid of telling the truth. I do this in the hope that it may be edifying to you. I do speak frankly with some hesitation because this revelation may cause many Christians to find reason to criticize and fall into a sense of self-righteousness; thereby failing to listen to the real message that God has for them in this chapter. Another concern would be that you stop reading at the end of this prelude and never read God's answer which comes in the next chapter. Above all, I want to caution you about not believing that there were not many moments of grace, joy and hope that carried me through all of those years. God always brought preachers, teachers, and revelations that guided me through each step and each moment. He showed me just enough of His Glory to keep me seeking more. To Him be the Glory and Praise.

Usually when I tell people that I accepted Christ as my Savior at the tender age of 5; they ask "How was it that even then, as a small child, I understood that I was a sinner and that I needed a savior?" I remember that when I accepted Christ, I was facing the corner in the kitchen looking at the light switch. I do not remember if I had been put there or if I had chosen to stand there. Dr. M. R. Dehaan's voice was coming across the radio. M. R. DeHaan, M.D. (1891-1965) was an American Bible teacher, pastor, author, physician, and founder of Radio Bible Class. One of his famous quotes was "Before an individual can be saved, he must first learn that he cannot save himself." He preached a lot about the blood of Christ for salvation. From that point onwards I tried to work hard enough for God and at walking this Christian life to deserve the salvation that I had been given. Despite the fact that I understood that salvation was by grace and faith, I somehow was trapped inside my own legalism. I kept placing myself back under the law for God's acceptance and love. As the chapter depicts, even at a young age, this was a struggle! When I started the first grade, I had a bad speech impediment and was overweight. Typically this was not a combination that attracts friends. In my case, I was laughed at a lot. However, you may want to know that I not only memorized a lot of scriptures at the age of 8 but by the age of 12, I was already a substitute Sunday school teacher. I was a Straight A student, liked by the teachers, and made fun of by the other children. Three years of speech therapy had erased my speech impediment, but left me with a European style accent while living in rural Missouri. I was overweight and shy. I poured all my effort into trying to please everyone around me. Interestingly, at the age of thirteen I lost all the weight, but no one seemed to notice that I was now slender.

My mother, though bipolar, had not yet been diagnosed. She always impressed upon me that the only occupation that God would honor for a woman was to be a wife and mother. When I was 16 and dating, she, driven by fear, would meet me at the doorway to interrogate me as to whether or not I was still a virgin. I was a virgin; but she seemed to not believe me. Not realizing that if I remained in my accelerated courses I was destined to graduate the Valedictorian, my father insisted that I change my courses to be a secretary. He said he could not send a daughter to college. So I changed my courses to please him and I got married to please my mother at age 16. I wanted to make them and God happy. Yet, I was miserable. I worked two part time jobs while finishing high school. Much of my time I spent in prayer and seeking God; but I was still unhappy. Along came another man who constantly complimented me and made me feel good about myself. I continued to tell him to go away because I was married and I drove myself further into prayer. I felt guilty for desiring to sin. Then one day, I exchanged desire for reality. At the young age of 18, I had an affair. I did not intentionally go out to displease God. I had not stopped going to church, praying or reading my Bible. In fact, I was diligently searching for God's help to keep me from sinning. Yet, I sinned. I became pregnant and knew immediately that the baby was the lover's baby; so, I did what I thought would be right. I divorced the first husband and married the father of the baby. In the meantime, the director of nursing at the hospital where I worked told me to either get an illegal abortion or leave. You see, the lover was Mexican and my husband had been a blonde. The town, in general, was very prejudiced and said it would be a disgrace to the community for any white American girl to marry a Mexican or bear his child. The church I attended told me to leave because I was a disgrace and a poor testimony to the young people. They did this without even asking me what was the truth or if I needed any counseling or help. I married my baby's father and I moved with him to Florida. All was well for a while. I continued to go to church, finished college to be a nurse, and loved my baby. My husband; however, was very jealous. One day he came home to tell me that he was having an affair (he now says only to get me to confess of having one myself); but, that day I left him.

By the age of 22, I was divorced twice and believed that surely God would never be able to use me now. Remember, I was still tied up in the belief that the only thing God would honor would be my being a successful, good wife. I was also trapped in the chains of guilt for my sins. I believed that I was a failure to God and He surely was repentant for having saved me. At age 24, I married Pedro Barba, the love of my life. He professed to be an atheist, but I was certain that with enough love; I would transform him. Actually, he did accept Christ as his Savior, 16 years later and nearly 6 months before his death. He was a brilliant doctor, but an undiagnosed bipolar. He could be the true Dr. Jekyll and Mr. Hyde in his behaviors; but, I loved him unconditionally. God used that marriage to begin to transform me and begin a steady process of teaching me about Grace and to tear down all those walls of legalism which had continued to rob me of the joy of my salvation. He taught me so much during those years that it would require a book of its own to tell that story. The most important thing He taught me was that He, God, loved me unconditionally.

Never during all those years had I openly looked at God to rebel. I actually wanted to please Him; yet, I seemed to have no idea how to because I was constantly trying to live the law in my own strength. I still did not understand that grace would set me free from all the bondage of sin that kept entangling me. Every difficulty or struggle, I saw as God's punishment to this failing and wayward child. Yet, my only desire was to please Him. The harder I tried, the more I failed. The more I failed, the greater my guilt became which circled back to my failing again. Occasionally, I seemed to triumph and my heart would leap with joy. And then I find myself falling back into that feeling that there must be something wrong with me and God could maybe save me; but never fully love me. Yet, God during all those years never let go of me and I never stopped seeking him.

Three years after Pete's death, I married again. This time I married a "professing Christian". Maybe this time God would bless me with a happy marriage. It wasn't long until I realized that this husband really only wanted my financial support. I paid thousands to fix his hunting cabin, paid off some of his debt, and gave him my van. He became angry because he wanted me to buy him a new truck and not give my sons cars. When I became sick with cancer, he began to regularly count up how much life insurance and social security he could draw if I died. During those difficult months of chemotherapy, he spent most of his time away at his hunting cabin. That was both a source of sorrow and relief. I knew that once more I was in a failed marriage. I really did not understand how this time. I begged God to guide me. I was not going to do anything this time until He told me to. Following the cancer I was diagnosed with ulcerative colitis. When I went for the total colectomy, my husband left on a hunting trip paid for out of my bank account. It was during that hospitalization that I wrote this chapter. This chapter came as an answer to my troubling question of what do I do with my own failure and guilt. So, I beg of you, do not stop here without the answer which follows.

Whiter Than Snow (Dealing with Guilt)

"though your sins be as scarlet, they shall be white as snow, though they be red like crimson, they shall be as wool." Isaiah 1:18

Throughout the majority of my life, I have struggled with my own sense of failure and guilt. This struggle predominately filled my thoughts when facing a trial. What did I do this time to deserve this punishment? Guilt and self-disdain would quickly change into utter despair. Then that despair at times led to a paralyzing depression which blocked my ability to accomplish anything or to feel love. In the center of this disdaining despair, I found that I could not feel God's presence; even though I know He was there. Everything appeared as though the world was crashing in around me and I was certain it must have been my fault. In those moments I became acutely aware of the fact that I would never be good enough to earn God's love by my own efforts. Though this is a struggle I have battled with during each valley; I do know that guilt is actually Satan's trap. Momentarily paralyzed in the grips of guilt, my testimony for Christ becomes nonexistent. In fact, anger builds within as I battle against guilt and self-hatred. In those moments of despair and anger, I have found myself plummeting downward farther and farther. That anger results in my snapping harsh words to those around me which then drives me ever deeper into despair. So, how can I or you be released from a sense of guilt and failure? The answer is to lay it forever at the cross of Christ and remember the fact that God has already paid for that sin. There are some direct consequences of sin which may result in trials; but God is not punishing you. For example, if I were to steal; then I might be in jail or if I decide to be promiscuous; then HIV may be a direct consequence of that decision. Yet, because Christ has covered my sins from the moment I accepted Him as my Savior; He can and will make something beautiful from even my failures when I bring them to the cross. Salvation is available by Grace and Grace alone. Although God may allow the consequences of my sin to occur; He is not standing up in heaven looking down waiting to swat me with some gigantic flyswatter. Instead, He looks down with great sorrow and tears over my failure to understand that His plan for me is the best. He knows that my failures are a result of my inability to fully comprehend His love and the price He paid for me.

My struggle with guilt and self-disdain has been my greatest thorn in the flesh. Even in childhood, I worked constantly striving toward perfection in hopes to be liked by those around me. I was an overweight little girl with a speech impediment; so, I worked hard toward pleasing the teachers and being a good student. I remember an incident in first grade. There was a little boy that I admired and he had used his crayons to color inside his desk. Since I thought his desk was so pretty, I decided to color inside mine. When the teacher angrily asked me who had colored my desk, I became frightened and said, "I don't know." Consequently, she paddled me and made me stay in during recess to clean my desk. This should have been the end of the story; but I carried around the guilt for the act and the lie for years. The remainder of that year, my eyes faced the floor whenever I had to go up front to answer a question or talk to the teacher. Inside, I felt that I was a failure; despite my graduating first grade as #1 in my class. Three years later, I remember some adult just to make conversation said, "You gotten spanked at school, yet?" Then quickly my little voice said "No." I was too ashamed to tell the truth; yet, I worried over that lie for many years to come. I somehow believed that God was going to reach down and strike me with a bolt of lightning. I have struggled with that same sense of fear and guilt throughout my life and even more so when a valley comes. Remember God's answer to Paul regarding his thorn in the flesh? God said, *"My grace is sufficient for thee: for my strength is made perfect in weakness"* 2 Corinthians 12:9. His Grace is sufficient to cover my failures, my sins and my guilt. He has gently reminded me of this truth each step of my journey. So, if you find yourself as a Christian burdened down by guilt; please take this journey with me. If you have never accepted Christ as your Savior, then also take this journey so as to find the only way to have your sin guilt removed.

When I first began my Master's program in late 1997, I would stay with my 104 year old Grandfather. He was essentially blind from macular degeneration and nearly deaf; yet, he lived alone and cared for himself. This patriarch of the faith spent every day in prayer and Bible study. He had special earphones and a taped Bible that he continued to study daily. I often joked that if I needed anything of God- I just needed to ask my Grandfather because I was certain he had a telephone to God, a direct hotline that never had any static. One of the times I was there he began to expound on Isaiah 1:18 *"though your sins be as scarlet, they shall be white as snow, though they be red like crimson, they shall be as wool."* He would tell me, as a reminder, that after accepting Christ, one's soul could no longer sin. The soul is made Whiter than snow. He would explain that our flesh could sin, but our soul could not sin. Our soul had been washed in the blood of Christ and would remain sinless from the moment we accepted Christ and throughout eternity.

Though I understood what this great Christian patriarch was saying, I failed to fully grasp the depth of those words or to accept the full gravity of their meanings. I understood with my intellect; yet, my own guilt would at times block this truth from my heart. The truth that we are made "whiter than snow" has such a depth of meaning and is the true expression of Grace demonstrated by God. Why do I fail to be able to claim this truth? Once more in these dark hours of despair; He has led me to look once more at this truth. I began to search the scripture about "white as snow". That review led me to find the other uses of "whiter than snow" or white as wool." That search led me to discover that those words were used in two separate references. It was used in referring to the leprosy of Miriam, Naaman, and Ghehazi. Then it was used in reference to Christ. At first there was some question in my mind as to how could the leprosy be used and at first I thought this had to be a mistake. Yet, God never makes a mistake; therefore I researched the references a little farther and then I found within the law an answer which I hope I might convey without causing any confusion. When looking at the law regarding leprosy we find in Leviticus 13: *¹²And if a leprosy break out abroad in the skin, and the leprosy cover all the skin of him that hath the plague from his head even to his foot, wheresoever the priest looketh; ¹³Then the priest shall consider: and, behold, if the leprosy have covered all his flesh, he shall pronounce him clean **that hath the plague: it is all turned white: he is clean.** ¹⁴But when raw flesh appeareth in him, he shall be unclean. ¹⁵And the priest shall see the raw flesh, and pronounce him to be unclean: for the raw flesh is unclean: it is leprosy."* So, if the flesh were all covered and had become all white (covering the diseased flesh); then the leper was declared clean. This is much like our sin being covered by the blood of Christ until the flesh below the surface of the white righteousness of Christ cannot be seen again in the eyes of God. The flesh is still there while we are on this earth, but it is completely covered by the blood of Christ and we are clothed in His white robes of righteousness—not ours, but His.

Now let's take a look at the scriptures about leprosy where "whiter than snow" were used.

Numbers 12

"¹And Miriam and Aaron spake against Moses because of the Ethiopian woman whom he had married: for he had married an Ethiopian woman. ²And they said, Hath the LORD indeed spoken only by Moses? hath he not spoken also by us? And the LORD heard it. ³(Now the man Moses was very meek, above all the men which were upon the face of the earth.) ⁴And the LORD spake suddenly unto Moses, and unto Aaron, and unto Miriam, Come out ye three unto the tabernacle of the congregation. And they three came out. ⁵And the LORD came down in the pillar of the cloud, and stood

in the door of the tabernacle, and called Aaron and Miriam: and they both came forth. ⁶And he said, Hear now my words: If there be a prophet among you, I the LORD will make myself known unto him in a vision, and will speak unto him in a dream. ⁷My servant Moses is not so, who is faithful in all mine house. ⁸With him will I speak mouth to mouth, even apparently, and not in dark speeches; and the similitude of the LORD shall he behold: wherefore then were ye not afraid to speak against my servant Moses? ⁹And the anger of the LORD was kindled against them; and he departed. ¹⁰And the cloud departed from off the tabernacle; and, behold, Miriam became leprous, white as snow: and Aaron looked upon Miriam, and, behold, she was leprous. ¹¹And Aaron said unto Moses, Alas, my lord, I beseech thee, lay not the sin upon us, wherein we have done foolishly, and wherein we have sinned. ¹²Let her not be as one dead, of whom the flesh is half consumed when he cometh out of his mother's womb. ¹³And Moses cried unto the LORD, saying, Heal her now, O God, I beseech thee. ¹⁴And the LORD said unto Moses, If her father had but spit in her face, should she not be ashamed seven days? let her be shut out from the camp seven days, and after that let her be received in again. ¹⁵And Miriam was shut out from the camp seven days: and the people journeyed not till Miriam was brought in again"

Miriam had sinned against God; yet when she was cursed with leprosy at the same time she was covered from head to toe. She was sent to separation from the group for seven days. She was aware of her sin and her leprous flesh; yet, He covered her white as snow which by the law would declare her clean. A perfect picture of Grace in that sinful flesh was covered white as snow by God's gracious hand. Before a person accepts the atonement for sin they must understand that they are a sinner and are in a sense "leprous with sin." Much like leprosy which destroys one's ability to feel pain; sin destroys overtime our ability to even feel any weight for our sins. One lie leads to bigger lies to full corruption sometimes with no remorse, etcetera.

The second example in which leprosy was used in the Bible with the words "whiter than snow" was very similar and as follows.

2 Kings 5: ²⁰But Gehazi, the servant of Elisha the man of God, said,

Behold, my master hath spared Naaman this Syrian, in not receiving at his hands that which he brought: but, as the LORD liveth, I will run after him, and take somewhat of him. ²¹So Gehazi followed after Naaman. And when Naaman saw him running after him, he lighted down from the chariot to meet him, and said, Is all well? ²²And he said, All is well. My master hath sent me, saying, Behold, even now there be come to me from mount Ephraim two young men of the sons of the prophets: give them, I pray thee, a talent of silver, and two changes of garments. ²³And Naaman said, Be content, take two talents. And he urged him, and bound two talents of silver in two bags, with two changes of garments, and laid them upon two of his servants; and they bare them before him. ²⁴And when he came to the tower, he took them from their hand, and bestowed them in the house: and he let the men go, and they departed. ²⁵But he went in, and stood before his master. And Elisha said unto him, Whence comest thou, Gehazi? And he said, Thy servant went no whither. ²⁶And he said unto him, Went not mine heart with thee, when the man turned again from his chariot to meet thee? Is it a time to receive money, and to receive garments, and oliveyards, and vineyards, and sheep, and oxen, and menservants, and maidservants? ²⁷The leprosy therefore of Naaman shall cleave unto thee, and unto thy seed for ever. And he went out from his presence a leper as white as snow."

Again though Gehazi's sin was displayed in the leprous flesh; God's Grace was displayed again by covering the entire flesh as white as snow—proclaiming Gehazi clean under the law. In both cases Miriam and Gehazi, lived out their days covered with this white flesh as a constant reminder of God's grace which can be a perfect illustration of our own exchange of our sin for Christ's righteousness. We must ever be reminded of who we really are (leprous sinners) saved by Grace and now covered with Christ's white robe of righteousness. Remembrance of our sins should not be as a result of "guilt" anymore; rather our clothing of righteousness should draw us ever more diligently in love to desire to display the righteousness in which we are clothed and not to demonstrate the flesh below. And we know that Gehazi was not retired from his service to God as one might note in 2 Kings 8: 4 where he is referred to as "Gehazi the servant of the man of God" That is the Grace of God fully demonstrated.

The remainder of the incidences in which God has used the expression of "whiter than snow" or "white as wool" are in reference to Christ Himself.

In Daniel 7:9 it is written *"And the Ancient of days did sit whose garment was white as snow and hair of his head like the pure wool."* Again in Matthew 28:3 when speaking of Jesus as he ascended from the grave *" His countenance was like lightening and his raiment white as snow, and the hair of his head like the pure wool."* Furthermore it is found in Matthew 28:3 when speaking of Jesus as he ascended from the grave *"His countenance was like lightening and his raiment white as snow."* It is amazing to me that there is a message found in these scriptures that have a greater importance than merely telling us about Saving Grace. The grace that saves us is already so much more than we deserve. This reference to "whiter than snow" is the key to understanding the Grace which sustains us. Understanding this Grace which sustains us is the key to gaining victory over our sinful flesh. Understanding this key principle does not give us the license to sin more; instead, it gives us the power to sin less by providing us the only Vicotry over sinful flesh, Christ Jesus and His power. In the remainder of the references to "white as snow" or in reference to wool, we can note that the scripture refers to the countenance of Christ. This is the Grace which carries us home one day. Though our sins are like "scarlet" when washed in the blood of Christ our souls take on "His image" and we become, as He is – sinless and blameless before God.

I also found this reference in Mark 9:3 as Peter, James and John transcended a high mountain *"He was transfigured before them. And his raiment became shining, exceeding white as snow, so as no fuller on earth can white them."* Christ's raiment was "whiter than snow" is also referred to in Revelations 1: 13-14 " *And in the midst of the candlesticks one like unto the Son of man his head and his hair were while like wool, as white as snow."*

Wow, when He says, "though your sins be as scarlet they shall be white as snow" He is referring to a transformation of our sins to being spotless like Jesus. Covered in His blood we are accounted as having perfection and become clothed with his white garment of righteousness. This is through faith and grace. Paul refers to Abraham in Romans 4:3, by saying *"Abraham believed God and it was counted unto him for righteousness."* Our faith and belief are counted for righteousness. *"Though your sins be as scarlet"-* refers to blood guiltiness. There are some who would try to say, "But I try to live a good life-I haven't done anything that bad." But as is noted in Romans 3:23 *"For all have sinned and fallen short of the glory of God."* None of us through works of our own can find righteousness or wash away our sin nature- we remain red as scarlet. Only the blood of Christ can make our garments "white as snow" *"But we are an unclean thing, and all our righteousnesses are as filthy rags; and we all do fade as a leaf; and our iniquities like the wind, have taken us away."* Isaiah 63:

Now Crimson is a red colorfast dye of the scarlet worm-it is a stain very difficult to eradicate. Therefore, the symbolic removal of this stain and turning it to white as wool represents something so difficult that man could not himself remove. It is a picture of the life changing Grace of God that delivers us from our sins. Our sins a deep stain impossible to remove is made white as wool by the precious blood of Christ.

This is truly of Grace and grace alone. *"For by Grace are ye saved through faith, and that not of yourselves it is the Gift of God-Not of works, lest any man should boast."* Ephesians 2:7-9 It is through faith that grace abounds unto righteousness. *"even so by the righteousness of one the free gift came upon all men unto justification of life. 19For as by one man's disobedience many were made sinners, so by the obedience of one shall many be made righteous."* Romans 5: 18-19

This righteousness that is accounted to each person who believes in Jesus Christ by faith is not based on works. Therefore, it cannot be a source of neither pride nor guilt. Our works cannot alter it. The soul is free from all sin-past, present and future. The soul becomes incapable of being covered with sin's stain. The soul cannot sin; though the flesh can. *"Whosoever is born of God doth not commit sin; for his seed remaineth in him: and he cannot sin, because he is born of God."* I John 3:9. When we are born we have the flesh and the spirit; but the soul is dead. It is the soul that becomes born at the point of salvation. For that reason, this reference refers to the second birth (the soul birth) which occurs during salvation. This perfection of the soul, this covering of our sins is forever due to the sacrifice of Christ. *"But this man, after he had offered the one sacrifice for sins forever, sat down on the right hand of God; from henceforth expecting till his enemies be made his footstool.* ***For by one offering he has perfected forever*** *them that are sanctified."* Hebrews 10: 12-14

It is difficult for us to recognize the magnitude of His Grace; but truly He has taken our scarlet stains of sin and washed them whiter than snow. He has made us sons-joint heirs of His kingdom. *"But when the fullness of time was come, God sent forth his Son, made of a woman, made under the law. To redeem them that were under the law, that we might receive the adoption of sons. And because ye are sons, God hath sent forth the Spirit of His Son into your hearts, crying Abba Father. Wherefore thou art no more a servant, but a son; and if a son, then an heir of God through Christ."* Galatians 4:4-7 Being covered by the blood of Christ, we are seen by the Father as "whiter than snow-like wool" just as He has described His Son. He is about the business of perfecting that transformation; yet, God always sees the finished product. *"For whom He did foreknow He also did predestinate to be conformed to the image of His Son"* Romans 8:29

At the point of accepting Christ as our Savior, we are forgiven of our sins. Additionally we are given Christ's righteousness-placed in our account. Being accounted righteous means we are no longer captives of neither guilt nor sin's hold. It has been my experience that when I get buried in my own guilt, I am more likely to keep falling into the same sin. Therefore, guilt does not release me from sin's hold on my life. Only grace and faith can do that. Besides, guilt is a very prideful thing when confronted with scripture. It is saying, "God, Christ may have died for my sin; but my sin is too big for God to forgive" or it is saying, "You may forgive me; but my standard of righteousness is so high I cannot forgive myself—my standard is therefore higher than God Almighty". When we are guilt-laden we are focused on our self and our sin rather than the blood of Christ. We do not become justified by wallowing in our guilt; we are justified by Christ. The truth of that sets you free from both sin and the guilt thereof. When you are condemning yourself, you are focused on you, not on God. 2 Corinthians 3: 17-18 says, "*¹⁷Now the Lord is that Spirit: and where the Spirit of the Lord is, there is liberty. ¹⁸But we all, with open face beholding as in a glass the glory of the Lord, are changed into the same image from glory to glory, even as by the Spirit of the Lord.*" So I urge you and myself to take our eyes off of our failures and look deep into the face of Christ.

Many fear to teach the truth concerning Grace. They fear that people will utilize this as a license to sin more. The truth gives too much liberty they think. Despite the inability of our soul to sin once saved- our flesh remains filled with the sin nature as is so clearly stated by Paul the apostle. "*For we know that the law is spiritual: but I am carnal sold under sin. For that which I do I allow not, for that which I would, that do I not, what I hate that I do. If then I do that which I would not, I consent unto the law that it is good. Now it is no more I that do it, but sin that dwelleth in me. For I know that in me (that is in my flesh) dwelleth no good thing for to will is present with me, but how to perform that which is good I find not. For the good that I would I do not but the evil which I would not, that I do. I find then a law, that, when I would do good, evil, is present with me. For I delight in the law of God after the inward man But I see another law in my members warring against the law of my mind and bringing me into the captivity to the law of sin which is in my members. O wretched man that I am who shall deliver me from the body of this death? I thank God through Jesus Christ our Lord. So then with the mind I myself serve the law of God, but with the flesh the law of sin.*" Romans 7: 15-25.

Our flesh, our sinful nature still sins: however the Holy Spirit which dwells in us draws us toward the likeness of Christ. *"There is therefore no condemnation to them which are in Christ Jesus, who walk not after the flesh, but after the Spirit. For the law of the Spirit of life in Christ Jesus hath made me free from the law of sin and death. For what the law could not do, in that it was weak through flesh, God sending his own Son in the likeness of sinful flesh and for sin condemned sin in the flesh, that the righteousness of the law might be fulfilled in us, who walk not after the flesh, but after the Spirit."* Romans 8:1-4. Once we take our focus off of our guilt and ourselves to place that focus on Jesus; we actually sin less. The reason being when we are focused on Christ, we see sin for what it really is-a barrier to demonstrating the praise to Christ that would bring Him the Glory we desire to bring Him. The more we focus on Christ, the more we love Him. The more we love Him, the more we want to bring smiles to His face rather than tears of sorrow. We become compelled by love to please Him, not out of fear.

My belated husband suffered greatly from a bipolar disorder which tormented him day and night. That spilled over at times to his becoming very abusive. The early years of my marriage led me to obey him out of fear. I remained frustrated, victimized, and doomed to fail over and over. There came a moment in which the eyes of my heart began to see him clearly as this tormented soul. Suddenly, my reason for trying to please him came out of love instead of fear. I wanted to ease his discomfort. No longer was I a victim. I was now empowered to love. I know in some ways this may be a poor illustration; yet, God used those years to teach me about unconditional love. He allowed me, this imperfect human, to demonstrate unconditional love. There I began to understand God's unconditional love for me which was greater than anything I could display. God does not have a bipolar abusive personality; but when we walk around with guilt and fear of His punishment, we are acting as though He does. Instead, He is looking at us with unconditional love which only wants the best for us.

What possibly can all this really mean to us? It means we have liberty and freedom from both guilt and worry concerning our Christian walk. It means that when I fall face down into the mud, God does not gleefully look down and rub my face in it. There in that pit of mud I may keep my head down as I pitifully cry out to God of my failure. At that very moment, God reaches down, takes my hand, and with gentle voice says as He looks through the blood of Christ; "What sin my child? I don't see any. Come. Take my hand. We have work that needs to be done. The fields are white with harvest." He gently pulls me up, dusts me off, kisses my cheek and off we go together. Such love and grace He displays. Indeed, this love draws us evermore to keep our eyes on Christ and our desire to sin and Satan's ability to tempt us fall to the wayside. We will not sin because our love and devotion to Christ will prevent it. When we take our eyes off of Christ and begin to "battle this sin ourselves, we will fall because once more we are looking at ourselves and not at Christ. Knowing that we are unworthy, why would we ever think that we can do anything to add to this salvation? Our victory over this sinful nature only comes when we are focusing on the only true righteousness which is Christ Jesus. Remember this salvation and this walk with God is dependent on faith and faith only. We are free from the bondage of the law. Let loose the chains that weigh you down. Accept God's full grace—knowing that once saved—your soul has been washed "whiter than snow". Let go of your chains of guilt and worry—allow the Holy Spirit to perform His work through you. Allow God's righteous work to be performed in your body by the Spirit. Take that deep breath of fresh air that fills your body and soul, that breath that comes from the freedom of walking in Grace. Oh, what Amazing and magnificent Grace that God hath poured forth on us.

Let us Pray

"Dear Heavenly Father, Thank you for your Grace that has covered all my sins. Thank you for the sacrifice of your Son that I might be freed forever from the bondage of sin, guilt and worry—that my soul might be "whiter than snow". My God thou art truly an awesome God, full of Mercy and Grace. Guide me with thy Spirit, direct my life. Let your righteousness Shine forth through me. Help me when I am weak and fail to claim this truth in my own life. Be my faith when I can no longer believe. Thank you for this love you have so freely given and thank you for your unconditional love even when I fail to love myself. In Jesus name I pray, Amen.

Therefore, Whiter than Snow
"Dealing with Guilt"

So, how do we lay aside the guilt? After all, we are guilty in our own effort and the only freedom is found through Christ. So, what are the steps we need to take with our failures so that we can be productive for Christ?

1. Lay your sin at the cross. If you have never before accepted Christ as your Savior, this is the first step. He died for your sins, rose again, and forever broke the chains that bind whoever accepts this sacrificial gift of love. If you know Christ as your Savior, bring your sin to Him. I John 1: *"⁹If we confess our sins, he is faithful and just to forgive us our sins, and to cleanse us from all unrighteousness."* Bringing our sin to Christ after salvation is not a part of our salvation (that was sealed when we accepted Christ as our Savior), but it is a very important part of our spiritual growth in this Christian Walk. The reason being that we need to see that sin for what it is-a barrier to our joy and peace in Christ. Sin fragments our ability to bring praise to Christ; because sin cannot Glorify Christ to the world. Sin fragments our ability to believe that God has a perfect plan of love for us. When we are living in sin, we do not demonstrate our love for God. Love means that we want to please the one loved. Love does not want to break the heart of the one we love. Sin breaks God's heart;

because in His omnipotence, God knows how sin will harm us. In His love, He wants what is best for each of his children. When we come to confess our sin, we are acknowledging that we see the sin as a separating point from God. When David confessed his sin with Bathsheba and Uriah, he asked God to restore unto him the joy of his salvation. David had finally seen the sin as breaking God's heart and came to him with a broken spirit with a broken and contrite heart. There is a difference in confessing from fear of punishment and confessing from a heart of love. When we confess from fear of punishment, we tend to fall back into the same sin. When we confess from a broken, contrite heart that loves Christ in all His Glory, we never want to cause Him sorrow again. Confess your sin to God as soon as you realize that you have sinned.

2. Study God's word diligently, morning and night. Psalm 119: "*11 Thy word have I hid in mine heart, that I might not sin against thee.*" Continue to study His word. Continue to listen to Bible teachers. Do not let your guilt cause you to run from Him into hiding. He knows exactly where you are. Seek to know Him. The more you know of Him, the more you will love Him. The more you love God, the less likely you are to sin against Him. Additionally, when you are drawn to sin, verses will come to your mind that cause you to halt before proceeding.

3. Quote these verses to yourself to remind you of the fact that He is working to complete the transformation of you into an image of Christ. He will finish that work. That is God's promise. Additionally, after accepting Christ, all His righteousness is accounted to your account. All His Glory He has chosen to share with you. These are the key verses, Romans 8, 2 Corinthians 3: 17-18, and the book of Galatians. Read these daily, pray them back to God until they are so written on your heart that the depths of their truth become a part of your spirit and transform your walk.

4. Remember God loves you and God chose you. When Christ went to the cross and all your sin and guilt were placed on His shoulders, He suffered suddenly the greatest agony that could ever be imagined when for a moment in time He was separated from the Father and the Holy Spirit. That agony was more severe than anything you or I might suffer on this earth and goes beyond the greatest agony that we can ever imagine. This He did willingly for you and for me. In his omniscience, He knew every sin that we would ever commit, every time that we would scorn Him, every time that we would doubt Him, and every time that we would deny Him. He still chose to die for you and to save you. He loved us that much. Never is there a sin in our life for which God says, "Oops, I didn't know I was forgiving THAT." Never does God say, "I am sorry I chose her (or him)." Please read Psalm 139. *¹O lord, thou hast searched me, and known me. ²Thou knowest my downsitting and mine uprising, thou understandest my thought afar off. ³Thou compassest my path and my lying down, and art acquainted with all my ways. ⁴For there is not a word in my tongue, but, lo, O LORD, thou knowest it altogether. ⁵Thou hast beset me behind and before, and laid thine hand upon me. ⁶Such knowledge is too wonderful for me; it is high, I cannot attain unto it. ⁷Whither shall I go from thy spirit? or whither shall I flee from thy presence? ⁸If I ascend up into heaven, thou art there: if I make my bed in hell, behold, thou art there. ⁹If I take the wings of the morning, and dwell in the uttermost parts of the sea; ¹⁰Even there shall thy hand lead me, and thy right hand shall hold me. ¹¹If I say, Surely the darkness shall cover me; even the night shall be light about me. ¹²Yea, the darkness hideth not from thee; but the night shineth as the day: the darkness and the light are both alike to thee. ¹³For thou hast possessed my reins: thou hast covered me in my mother's womb. ¹⁴I will praise thee; for I am fearfully and wonderfully made: marvellous are thy works; and that my soul knoweth right well. ¹⁵My substance was not hid*

from thee, when I was made in secret, and curiously wrought in the lowest parts of the earth. ¹⁶Thine eyes did see my substance, yet being unperfect; and in thy book all my members were written, which in continuance were fashioned, when as yet there was none of them. ¹⁷How precious also are thy thoughts unto me, O God! how great is the sum of them! ¹⁸If I should count them, they are more in number than the sand: when I awake, I am still with thee. ¹⁹Surely thou wilt slay the wicked, O God: depart from me therefore, ye bloody men. ²⁰For they speak against thee wickedly, and thine enemies take thy name in vain. ²¹Do not I hate them, O LORD, that hate thee? and am not I grieved with those that rise up against thee? ²²I hate them with perfect hatred: I count them mine enemies. ²³Search me, O God, and know my heart: try me, and know my thoughts: ²⁴And see if there be any wicked way in me, and lead me in the way everlasting.

5. Remember this, God never lets go of you.

6. Hold tight to the truth that God's plan for you is perfect. This omniscient, omnipotent, omnipresent God designed a plan of love for you to bring you to a place of joy, hope and peace in Him.

7. When Satan torments you with guilt for your past, tell him to, "Go away, my Father already paid the price and point Satan to the cross and the resurrection"

8. Do Not dwell in the bad of the past. Remember God's graces and mercies that led you through. As Paul says in Philippians 3: *"¹²Not as though I had already attained, either were already perfect: but I follow after, if that I may apprehend that for which also I am apprehended of Christ Jesus. ¹³Brethren, I count not myself to have apprehended: but this one thing I do, **forgetting those things which are behind**, and reaching forth unto those things which are before, ¹⁴I press toward the mark for the prize of the high calling of God in Christ Jesus."*

I wish that I could tell you that after God answered my plea by giving me the truths in this chapter, I never again fell prey to my guilt and never again fell to the same lies. It was a step forward in the transformation that many years later led to my writing "A Broken and Contrite Heart" Since then, I have found peace and rest in the love of God. I am Christ's bride and do not need anything or anyone else to be loved. There are other things for which I stumble now whenever I take my eyes off of Christ; but, I have finally learned that the only power to live this Christian life is found in Christ. He who made the impossible exchange of His righteousness for my sin is the truest love of my life and I love Him more each day. His mercy, His love, His pursuit of me, His character and His Glory have drawn me to love Him.

What did God do with all my failures? Well the last husband came to tell me of an affair he had to demonstrate how other women wanted him; so I did get a divorce and changed my name back to Barba. A few years later, I saw his son who told me that because of my testimony he had accepted Christ as his Savior. He apologized for his father and said, "I know how my father treated you and the pain he caused, I am sorry. But remember this, God sent you into my life so I could find Him. Thank you." Pedro Barba accepted Christ as his Savior six months before he died, an eternity was changed. From that marriage Alberto and Ronald were born; God's gift of mercy to me and to the world who would meet them. How many lives have been transformed because of the testimony of my sons. Melissa, my beautiful daughter was born from the previous marriage. She is my delight and my best friend. Her spirit transforms all around her. Sadly, the hospital went bankrupt shortly after their demanding I get an abortion or leave (I had left). The church, which had thrown me out without even seeking to counsel me, divided and split within a year because of disagreements amongst its members. Never forget God can take all your sins and when you lay them at His feet, He can change them into something beautiful. Knowing that depth of love from Him, how could I ever want to break His heart with my sin? Rest assured in His arms of love.

Prelude for Giving When I Have Nothing Left to Give

After so many years of constantly climbing against the obstacles of illness, finances, and self defeat; I had reached a point in 2002 of emotional, spiritual, and physical fatigue that left me feeling drained every evening. The multiple trips to St. Louis for endoscopic ultrasounds and biopsies of the pancreas had ended with no real answer; except the questionable diagnosis of Chronic Autoimmune Pancreatitis. I was working in Springfield, MO as a hospitalist Nurse Practitioner and part-time as a nurse to keep the bills paid (my total hours were about 60 hours a week). Each morning I would get up, drink my coffee—study my Bible, a time in prayer, and off to work I would go. Once there I would smile, care for the patients, profess of God's love and grace, and then I would go home where I would close my doors. Once home I threw down my sword and cried at God's feet. In the quietness of my apartment I would listen to sermons or study my Bible and collapse into bed with a prayer that God would give me the strength again tomorrow not to fail to testify of Him. So often, I could feel His arms around me during those nights to restore me for the next day. Sometimes I would awaken about two or three in the morning with some song playing in my memory (always the right song for the moment) lulling me back into a peaceful sleep. My time to rest and be alone with God was essential to my continuing to work because my health was quite fragile (much like it is now) The difference between then and now is that back then

I still had wanted someone who would be there to share my burden and take care of me. Now I am quite at peace knowing that God is the only companion I need. Additionally, I am more willing to accept myself with my frailties and for that reason I am not quite as hard on myself for my inabilities to keep everything done. I marveled that God would carry me through each day in spite of my fatigue and my health problems; but I felt that each day I had not even a drop of energy left for anything else. That was when suddenly I was required to take on the care of Mom.

It was mid to late 2002 when my mother had a sudden collapse in mental health. She is bipolar with psychotic features and suddenly she had an exacerbation of her disease. I made multiple trips the 4 hours back to Dexter to take her to the psychiatrist and return back to get ready for work the next day. Finally I decided that all these efforts were to no avail. She continued to remain completely off balance and would call me almost daily to tell me that she was afraid she might harm herself or her cats. So, I brought her back to Springfield and had her admitted into the mental hospital. Then, with the help of my nephew I moved her essential things to an independent living apartment I had found for her very close to my apartment.

During the time from 1994 to 2000 when I and the children had lived in Dexter, she had come over to cook their breakfast, do their laundry, and cook their dinner every day while I was getting my Master's Degree and battling cancer. She had also bought my house, contributed great financial support, and drove over whenever I called. I know that all of this was a great sacrifice for her; but at the moment of her collapse the only sentence that kept ringing in my ears was "I will be glad when you and your kids are gone so I can have my peace." I realize now that she had only said that at a moment of frustration when feeling unappreciated for her sacrifice; but often as humans we can be so focused on ourselves that we don't see the other person's needs. I know that there are some statements I have made to my children that I only pray they don't remember or at least have come to forgive me for having blurted them out. Beyond that, remember that Satan loves to play back recording in your head to cause conflict, confusion or doubt. Still for that moment in 2002 that recording kept playing in my head while Mom complained about my moving her to Springfield and saying to anyone who would listen, "My daughter stole everything from me and made me move here."

My mother was frightened and upset by the fact that suddenly everything she had owned was narrowed down to what could fit in an apartment. She did send me back to Dexter weekly to pick up another list of items until there was not any more room to put her stuff. She then rented out her house and later sold it. She was caught in the conflict between needing me, fear for her future (could she trust me to take care of her?), and frustration with our differences in personality. I was also caught in that same conflict. I was barely able to take care of myself, go to work and be available whenever my children needed me. How was I going to have the strength or the energy to take care of Mom? I was tired, I was sick, I was financially in a dark hole, and Satan kept playing multiple tapes that blurred my vision. I wanted to help Mom, but I was frustrated, lonely and wanting someone to take care of me. I couldn't remember the last time a human being had put their arms around me and said, "It is ok, I love you and everything is going to be ok. Well, with the exception that my children, I can't remember anyone ever doing that. My children would have been there for me again; except, I did not want to burden them with my trials. That was when I wrote this chapter.

Giving When I Have Nothing Left to Give

Psalm 121: "*¹I will lift up mine eyes unto the hills, from whence cometh my help.*
²My help cometh from the LORD, which made heaven and earth."

I find myself once more in the depths of a despairing valley. My only hope is to cry out to God as did David, "*¹Hear my cry, O God; attend unto my prayer. ²From the end of the earth will I cry unto thee, when my heart is overwhelmed: lead me to the rock that is higher than I. ³For thou hast been a shelter for me, and a strong tower from the enemy. ⁴I will abide in thy tabernacle for ever: I will trust in the covert of thy wings. Selah.*"

I pleaded, "Oh, my Dear Heavenly Father, please bring me into thine arms and let me abide there until this storm passes over. My mind is circling inside of my head. It is so hard to even think clearly; yet, I know that thou art able to calm the storm inside of me and it is that promise and that truth to which I cling when everything around me and inside of me feels the whirlwind of doubt. Be my faith for mine is crumbling. Lord please be my joy, for all I feel is despair. Help me Lord to feel your Love, so that I might then share your love to those whom I need to take care of, particularly Mom. I need Your strength Lord; because I am worn out. My strength is gone. I need Your fountain of flowing water to fill my thirsty and parched soul. I feel Lord that I have nothing left to give; so please fill me up with You."

God had destined me in life to be a giver. My spiritual gift was that of Mercy. This gift was so well handpicked by God so that I would be the caregiver to Pete, my children, and my patients. Many people passed through my life that became for time periods also recipients of my care. When I was younger and healthier, I loved this part of my life. Three years of chronic illness and being pressed to support myself while at the same time paying off the bills left after the years of illness had taken its toll. At that time, I felt so alone on this earth; despite having God and my family. My children were grown and off to college. I knew that God was there and present. I particularly would feel His presence during the night or feel His breath in the soft wind blowing in the evening. Still I was tired from the journey and uncertain whether I could truly demonstrate Christ while taking on one more task. There seemed to be no energy left for giving of myself to anyone in need. So I had to turn to the scripture to find some way to keep moving forward with the help of my Savior.

In Matthew 28:20 Christ promised, "*lo, I am with you always, even unto the end of the world. Amen.*" What a thought, the Great I am, creator of the Universe has promised to always be with me. How could I ever feel alone? When my strength leaves me, He reminds me that "*13I can do all things through Christ which strengtheneth me.*"Philippians 4. He also reminds me that He will be my strength, requiring no energy of my own. This fact is shown in Isaiah 40: "*28Hast thou not known? hast thou not heard, that the everlasting God, the LORD, the Creator of the ends of the earth, fainteth not, neither is weary? there is no searching of his understanding. 29He giveth power to the faint; and to them that have no might he increaseth strength. 30Even the youths shall faint and be weary, and the young men shall utterly fall: 31But they that wait upon the LORD shall renew their strength; they shall mount up with wings as eagles; they shall run, and not be weary; and they shall walk, and not faint.*" The eagle soars effortlessly. All I have to do is wait on Him. And whenever my soul feels parched, I am reminded in John 4:14 where Christ declared, "*14But whosoever drinketh of the water that I shall give him shall never thirst; but the water that I shall give him shall be in him a well of water springing up into everlasting life.*" The chemotherapy that I had gone through made my ability to remember the scripture, chapter and verse nearly impossible. Yet, my Bible was marked from the years of reading it and I had found Gateway Bible on the internet to help me find the promises. Beyond that, God had promised me the Comforter to be my memory and to even pray for what I never knew to pray for. This was Christ's promise in John 14: *12Verily, verily, I say unto you, He that believeth on me, the works that I do shall he do also; and greater works than these shall he do; because I go unto my Father. 13And whatsoever ye shall ask in my name, that will I do, that the Father may be glorified in the Son. 14If ye shall ask any thing in my name, I will do it. 15If ye love me, keep my commandments. 16And I will pray the Father, and he shall give you another Comforter, that he may abide with you for ever; 17Even the Spirit of truth; whom the world cannot receive, because it seeth him not, neither knoweth him: but ye know him; for he dwelleth with you, and shall be in you. 18I will not leave you comfortless: I will come to you. 19Yet a little while, and the world seeth me no more; but ye see me: because I live, ye shall live also. 20At that day ye shall know that I am in my Father, and ye in me, and I in you…25These things have I spoken unto you, being yet present with you. 26But the Comforter, which is the Holy Ghost, whom the Father will send in my name, he shall teach you all things, and bring all things to your remembrance, whatsoever I have said unto you.*"

If now by the providence and direction of God, I must take on the duty of taking care of my mother; then, I should never worry about how to do it. His promise again in John 14 was, "*27Peace I leave with you, my peace I give unto you: not as the world giveth, give I unto you. Let not your heart be troubled, neither let it be afraid.*" He who envelopes me in His arms of love can also provide me with the love I need to give each day. He is my love provider, my passion, my hope, my joy and my strength. Paul in 2 Corinthians relates, "*5Of such an one will I glory: yet of myself I will not glory, but in mine infirmities. 6For though I would desire to glory, I shall not be a fool; for I will say the truth: but now I forbear, lest any man should think of me above that which he seeth me to be, or that he heareth of me. 7And lest I should be exalted above measure through the abundance of the revelations, there was given to me a thorn in the flesh, the messenger of Satan to buffet me, lest I should be exalted above measure. [8]For this thing I besought the Lord thrice, that it might depart from me. [9]And he said unto me, My grace is sufficient for thee: for my strength is made perfect in weakness. Most gladly therefore will I rather glory in my infirmities, that the power of Christ may rest upon me. [10]Therefore I take pleasure in infirmities, in reproaches, in necessities, in persecutions, in distresses for Christ's sake: for when I am weak, then am I strong."* Though I may have lost my physical strength and I may at times feel that I have nothing left within me, I too like Paul realize that my weakness merely drives me to the cross; where Christ can become my strength, my love, and my hope. I am forced to stop trying to do His work in my strength and must do it in His. All of what I thought was important fades in comparison to knowing Him. Philippians 3: *"[7]But what things were gain to me, those I counted loss for Christ. [8]Yea doubtless, and I count all things but loss for the excellency of the knowledge of Christ Jesus my Lord: for whom I have suffered the loss of all things, and do count them but dung, that I may win Christ, [9]And be found in him, not having mine own righteousness, which is of the law, but that which is through the faith of Christ, the righteousness which is of God by faith:"* Nothing compares to the grand opportunity of knowing Christ intimately, passionately as my friend, my brother, my companion and my Savior. My prayer is that I might savor Him and seek Him no matter what my physical circumstance. As that happens I will love Him even more and He will become that precious sweet joy that overflows through me and to those whom He has placed in my charge. 2 Corinthians 2: *"[14]Now thanks be unto God, which always causeth us to triumph in Christ, and maketh manifest the savour of his knowledge by us in every place. [15]For we are unto God a sweet savour of Christ"*

My triumph in any situation is not dependent upon me. It is completely dependent upon God. Through each trial he gives us the sweet savor of knowing Him more which can overflow through us to all around us. Let me please take the liberty to quote from the Amplified Version 2 Corinthians 2: 14-16 *"[14]But thanks be to God, Who in Christ always leads us in triumph [as trophies of Christ's victory] and through us spreads and makes evident the fragrance of the knowledge of God everywhere, ¹⁵For we are the sweet fragrance of Christ [which exhales] unto God, [discernible alike] among those who are being saved and among those who are perishing: ¹⁶To the latter it is an aroma [wafted] from death to death [a fatal odor, the smell of doom]; to the former it is an aroma from life to life [a vital fragrance, living and fresh]. And who is qualified (fit and sufficient) for these things? [Who is able for such a ministry? We?]"*

My dear Heavenly Father, I bow in awe of Your Grace and Your sufficiency. Whenever I in my frailty seek refuge, You are there. When I am unable, Thou art more than able to accomplish Your work through me. Let me seek Your face. Let me rest assuredly in Your promises. Keep me ever close and my eyes focused on You. Be my faith when mine fails me. Guide each and every servant of Yours to this truth, this promise, this place of rest. Prepare us each and every one to perform the task that we think is too difficult. It is in the blessed name of Jesus that we ask this, knowing that anything that we ask in His name shall be done. Thank you in the name of Jesus, Amen.

Therefore Giving When You Have Nothing Left to Give

So, now how do you and I perform these acts of giving when we feel we are too drained of all energy to move forward? We must learn, step by step to rely on Christ for the strength. You might think that this task is too difficult and easier said than done. These are the steps that I have learned to use and continue learning to use. My health is at best tedious, my work is a very demanding type job requiring from 60 to occasionally 70 hours in a week, and my mother now lives with me and needs ever increasing help as she ages. By the way, there were more tape recordings in my brain that have finally become silenced. Mom and I have lived together 8 years and though I will not tell you there were no conflicts and trials along the way for both of us; but I and Mom have reached a much better understanding of each other. We do love and accept each other without conditions. In addition to mom, I have a variety of rescued cats that require my care and one rescued dog. So here is how I keep this schedule.

1. Each morning when I awaken, I spend at least 30 minutes in bed talking to God about the day before and the day ahead. I do this in bed because my household will begin calling to me the minute they know I am up; so, God and I have a conversation first about everything that is going on.
2. Once out of bed, I listen to at least 2 sermons via the internet and post a Bible Verse for my friends on facebook to read.

3. So, to accomplish this, feed the animals and mom, get ready for work I do get up very early. Still I am very protective of my sleep which is important. I am in bed by 8pm and do not answer any phones unless it is my children. I pray a good night prayer to God after studying His Word.

4. Also, though I am not always the best at this one, I recognize that I do better if I get on the treadmill every morning during one of the sermons—so I am currently reforming that habit. Exercise is important.

5. When I start the self pity cycle, I never let myself stay there too long. Self pity is sin because it means I have taken my eyes off of Christ and am only looking at me. When that starts I listen to John Piper's Audio books and joyous Christian praise while asking God to refocus me. Whenever I do not recover immediately by these means I go back to the Psalm and say with David, "My time is in Your hands" My time for sorrow, my time for pain, my time for joy and my time for hope are all in Your hands. Hold me close in Your arms and carry me until such a time as You choose to restore my hope and my joy. Then I keep going.

6. I break down the tasks to smaller ones—never look at the whole picture which can defeat you. Ask for help from God to keep going for the next hour and then the next hour and then the next hour until the day is completed and then thank Him

This has been the steps I take which have kept me leaning on Jesus all the way. Well, not really my steps exactly but how God has demonstrated His Guidance by the help of the Holy Spirit every step of the way. I have had several surgeries since the initial writing in 2003 and I still have Chronic Autoimmune Pancreatitis which is taking a physical toll on my body; yet, God's love and Grace continue to carry me through. Whenever I am dealing with pain, I have refused to take narcotics beyond the first month post-op as I knew my own body would produce endorphins if I left it to work on its own. I have refused antidepressants, as I recognized that my moments of depression were only situational and would pass. I do not say that these medications do not have a role in helping people nor do I condemn those who need them; but I do caution you as to their many bad side effects and their ability to blur your ability to think clearly. There are those who require medications such as these; but proceed with prayer and caution when you do. Some have severe chemical imbalances which require medications; so to all of you—don't stop taking them because of how I feel for them and always seek medical help to guide you in this.

The most important thing is to take your eyes off of all your own inadequacies and place your eyes on Christ. Remember this entire lifetime is but a moment or blink of an eye compared to an eternity in Christ. He has the strength to perform whatever task He has given you here on earth and He will walk each step of the way with you. As you seek Him and keep your eyes focused on Him, His love will draw you ever closer to Him where strength, hope, peace and joy abound.

Prelude to Loneliness

Loneliness is a state of mind where one feels isolated and often misunderstood. There seems to be no one who truly understands or shares exactly the feelings of the spirit and soul with you. No one understands or shares your agony, your sorrow, your joys, nor what you are trying to say. Loneliness is the intense realization that there is no other person who intimately knows one's very thoughts, feelings, hopes, dreams, joys, tragedies, and there remains a constant search for just one person who might take the time to really know you and still love you. The existentialists believe that actually this is the plight of every human being ever born. That same search may lead to failed relationships, despair, constant running from one social event to another, drug usage, alcohol—anything to numb that feeling for a moment.

I am certain that anyone who has read my book this far would recognize that the sense of loneliness was a crippling force to me in my Christian walk from a very young age. Little did I know or understand the true causes and thereby I was a long time finding the solution despite the answer being in the Bible all of the time.

I have been told that even as a small toddler I had a complex personality. My mother said that I would be in the floor playing with my brother. When he would steal my toy I would protest to him; however, when my mother would come in to intervene—suddenly I would say, "No mom, it's ok. He can have that toy, I don't want it." I did not want her to punish him. We were both born in 1954—he was born in February and I prematurely was born in December. We lived on a farm about 6 miles from the nearest town and at least ½ mile from any neighbors. Because of the solitude, Charlie was my best friend. When he left for school one year before me I felt very alone. I wanted to go to school. That was the year I gained a lot of weight and went from slender to quite obese. I guess it was the beginning of covering my emotions with food. When it finally became my turn to start school the next year, I was very tall, overweight, and had a speech impediment—not the best combination in the first grade for anyone. I was also intellectually ahead of my class and made straight A's, since I had studied alongside my brother when mom was trying to help him. So I left for school, excited and hopeful only to begin to learn how cruel children can be. Certainly, I was made fun of, chosen last for any sport and made to go last in line on the playground. When we had physical education and played red rover the chant would be, "Red Rover, Red Rover—send fatty on over." At jump rope the girls would say, "Pretty first, fat last." I will never forget the one girl, Toni Keirsey, who spoke back and said, "Pretty is as pretty does." I also remember in first grade one little boy who really seemed behind in the class as if he really did not understand. He constantly got into trouble and was paddled by the teacher. I would sit there and feel so much pain for him; I wanted to scream out, "Don't you see he doesn't want to be bad, he just doesn't understand." My brother also got into trouble several times during grade school. Some of the time, I was actually a bystander on two or three occasions; knew that he had been wrongly accused and taken to the principal's office to be paddled. I got scared and said nothing until I got home and did tell mom and dad that the teacher was wrong. She had not seen what happened and I had. Throughout my childhood, I had this very empathetic, complex personality who felt no one really understood all these emotions that I had. I did memorize Bible scripture and pray; but I did not understand this intimate relationship with God. In fact, I wished I could hide all my flaws from Him; since, I thought He might despise me too. He had saved me by the blood of His Son, but perhaps He did not really like me too much and was standing there with paddle in hand.

The ducks, the cats and the dog became my best friends. In our household, hugging was not done. Mom had never been hugged as a child and just didn't have it in her to do so. (I later determinedly changed that with my children.) My father was a big, strong farmer with little education and demonstrated his love by working day and night. He felt awkward hugging his children, so he didn't. Thus was my life and even into high school. I had lost the weight, but no one noticed that I was attractive. I wanted to be nominated for queen and instead I was known as the brain and the walking Bible. My strong stand on God's principles and His word kept me fenced away from the popular crowd. When I married at 16 to please my mother, I became the joke of the school. Despite my being a virgin when I married the usual taunts were, "The preacher must be pregnant, that is why she got married." No one, not even my parents really knew me—I bottled it all up inside and kept right on marching forward to work, to school and to the day ahead.

Throughout my adult life I always wanted to find that one person who would love me unconditionally, know me intimately—even my very thoughts, and stand beside me through every tragedy, joy, hope, success, ruin, health and pain in this life. So by 2003 with all the failures behind, one would think I had learned the truth. Actually, despite all the Bible Study and all the growth spiritually, I was still lacking in this one of the most important lessons of why so much loneliness. This chapter was perhaps the beginning of my definitive search for the answer. So long I thought it was something wrong with me. I had not known the truth. Bouts of loneliness are the plight of every human being who has not learned the truth about our original purpose and relationship with God. Hopefully, I can explain this further as you go through the remainder of this section on Loneliness.

Loneliness

" ⁸I have set the LORD always before me: because he is at my right hand, I shall not be moved.

⁹Therefore my heart is glad, and my glory rejoiceth: my flesh also shall rest in hope.

¹⁰For thou wilt not leave my soul in hell; neither wilt thou suffer thine Holy One to see corruption.

¹¹Thou wilt shew me the path of life: in thy presence is fulness of joy; at thy right hand there are pleasures for evermore. Psalms 16: 8-11

One of my most devastating failures as a Christian comes to mind when I think of my moments of loneliness. Shouldn't I be content with all that God has given me or has done for me? Have you ever felt like you have always been lonely? I have at times felt deep pains of jealousy when I see a woman who appears to have a husband who loves her adoringly, gives selflessly, and protects her. Throughout my lifetime, this great flaw of mine, I have kept well hid from the people around me. I am embarrassed or scared to let people know how I really feel- like an introverted, misunderstood, outcast. The truth is I am successful a lot of the time at fooling myself as well until I get alone inside my apartment. I learned throughout my youth how to turn off that part of me and transform into the warm, friendly, gracious, strong person

I portrayed at work and in the public eye. In that transformation, I really became able to win others to Christ, to teach the Bible and to be successful at work. During that transformation, my feelings, thoughts and actions are very genuine. I knew the truth of who God was and believed that He performed the transformation because I handed it to Him. That is partially true; but why then did the loneliness return when He and I were alone in the confines of my apartment. So this would lead me to wonder at times whether I was just a phony because this loneliness would return. I had tried going "out with the girls" and still felt like I didn't belong. I found no real comfort in what seemed to be vain conversation. Even in the church, I stood alone so often. I have helped people, tried charity, teaching and still had this returning sense of loneliness which plagued me.

I am a Nurse Practitioner and my day is very fulfilling in that I am able to reach out and touch so many hearts. I find great pleasure in giving and in comforting a frightened soul or reaching out in true love to touch someone who is hurting. Truly, the nurses and co-workers who seem to genuinely care for me bless me with their smiles and their invitations. God has truly given me the best of the best in my co-workers, bosses, and comrades. Yet, there are times I wish that when I go home there would be someone there waiting with open arms to receive me. Particularly, now when I am facing an uncertainty and a road that may be wrought with pain and suffering. If I have pancreatic cancer; how, can I face this alone? I still remember how hard it was with the chemotherapy and with the previous surgeries. I remember how painful those moments could be. The loneliest moment of all had occurred after the total colectomy. There was a two month period in which I had a double-barrel ileostomy (a portion of the small intestine is brought to the surface and place on the outside of the abdomen and then split into two parts that can later be reconnected.) Because of all my previous surgeries the placement of this was difficult and the bags frequently broke or came off. Particularly this would occur every night in the middle of the night. Ileostomies are the small intestine, so are constantly moving forward; unlike the colon which is made to store. That meant that stool was constantly oozing out. Once the bag broke, I would awaken lying in a pool of feces. After a shower and a change of the pads I covered my bed with, I would go about the arduous task of trying to prep the skin and replace the bag. That would sometimes seem an impossible task as I could never get the skin free of liquid feces long enough to get the bag on. I remember the long and lonely hours when at three in the morning I would sit in a cold bedroom shivering, crying and so sick trying to replace that bag with no one there to hold me or even care. When I think back to those moments, I wonder if I have the strength to do it all again through whatever this pancreatic mass is.

It is in those moments that I cry forth to God and wonder why I must be alone. Am I unworthy of true love? I've spent a lifetime taking care of everyone around me, putting myself secondary to the needs of others and yet; I have not been given this one desire. There are those moments when I feel I have nothing left, no valor, no strength, and no love to give anymore. Yet, it is in those still small moments alone with God that He comes and reminds me of His presence and strength. In those moments of dark despair I fall before His throne and become wrapped in His love. I have been falling before His throne for a long time.

Even when my husband Pete was alive, he was not able to demonstrate love for he was wrapped in a great deal of pain from his childhood. This I understood and tried to accept valiantly. I knew he needed the love and the silent loneliness of my spirit was the sacrifice that God required of me. I did it like a diligent soldier—waiting for that moment of victory when everything would change. Only hours before he died, he told me of the depths of love that he truly felt for me. He told me I was the only good and pure thing that had ever been in his life. He said that he trusted me with all my strength and faith to take care of his sons and that I was the best mother he knew. I told him that I was too weak and frail. I needed his strength and his love. Then 8 hours later he was dead. I had waited our entire marriage for those words and now once I had received them, God took him away from me. I looked into the heavens and said, "Why, God, Why now?"

Throughout the Bible, God has provided us with examples of times when His people have had to spend many years in loneliness and even exile. One of those was David. For many years he was forced to run through the lands in fear of his life as Saul sought to kill him. Despite the people throughout this time that were there to help him, he felt very much alone. He cried out to God in this state of loneliness—"*Unto thee will I cry, O Lord my rock: be not silent to me: lest, if thou be silent to me, I become like them that go down into the pit. Hear the voice of my supplications, when I cry unto thee, when I lift up my hands toward they holy oracle*" *Psalm 28: 1-2* He then almost immediately hears Gods answer and concludes, "*Blessed be the Lord, because he hath heard the voice of my supplications. The Lord is my strength and my shield; my heart trusted in him, and I am helped: therefore my heart greatly rejoiceth; and with my song will I praise him. The Lord is their strength and he is the saving strength of his anointed.*" *Psalm 28:6-8*. Indeed he spoke of God's help through his tumultuous times as he sang, "*Thou hast turned for me my mourning into dancing: thou hast put off my sackcloth, and girded me with gladness; to the end that my glory may sing praise to thee, and not be silent. O Lord my God: I will give thanks unto thee for ever.*" Psalm 30:11-12.

It is in those moments of our deepest sense of loneliness that we find that we are not alone, for God himself is there with us. He promised, "*I will pray the Father, and he shall give you another comforter that he may abide with you for ever; Even the Spirit of truth whom the world cannot receive because it seeth him not, neither knoweth him; but ye know him; for he dwelleth with you, and shall be in you. I will not leave you comfortless; I will come to you. Yet a little while; and the world seeth me no more; but ye see me; because I live, ye shall live also. At that day ye shall know that I am in my Father, and ye in me, and I in you.*" John 14: 16-20.

It is in this truth, I am never alone. I have the greatest companion imaginable, for it is the arms of Christ that I am able to lean on in times of distress. This is the truth that Joseph knew when his own brothers sold him into slavery. It is this truth that Daniel held when thrown into the Lion's Den. It was Christ who stood in the fiery furnace with Shadrach, Meshach and Abednego. Therefore, we are never alone.

This is the truth that provided the Apostle Paul solace when he sat in the prison cell. He knew that he was not alone there. In fact, in those dungeons, he found strength, hope, and faith. Those lonely hours were not lonely but a place where he gained strength from God to perform the mission he was sat out to complete. In the dark and lonely places he found hope, joy, love, and peace because he had learned this promise given us by Jesus Christ.

It is from this prison cell that Paul writes us some of his greatest epistles including Ephesians, Philippians, Philemon and Colossians. It was from the prison that he wrote, *"Rejoice in the Lord always and again I say, Rejoice Be careful for nothing; but in prayer and supplication with thanksgiving let your requests be made known unto God and the peace of God, which passeth all understanding, shall keep your hearts and minds through Christ Jesus."* Phillipians 4:4-7. He knew true joy in the presence of Christ there in a prison cell.

It is this truth that rids me of my loneliness and indeed causes me now to treasure my moments of aloneness with him. Despite the fact that my children are grown and my house would appear empty, truly I am no longer alone there. Certainly, if I choose to come home and never speak to Him, I may feel lonely for a moment; but if I call upon Him, He will give me the comfort and companionship that I seek. It has reached the point in my life that even if I fail to call upon Him and I pass the evening feeling sorry for myself, when I go to sleep, He calls to me. Sometimes in the words of a song, sometimes in His quiet presence He makes His presence known to me. It is there that I regain the strength to face the morning and the next day whatever may come. I have found that for me the aloneness with Him is necessary so as to keep my eyes focused on my true love. He is ever present with me.

It is in those moments alone with Him that I find that I am able to drop my sword, fall down upon my face and cry unashamedly to Him. He alone I can tell of my frailty and my fears. He in those moments is able to take my trembling shoulders within His arms and give me true peace. My sorrow may last for the nighttime, but He is truly able to turn my mourning into great joy. It is in His presence, I find love and fulfillment.

Perhaps I can demonstrate this better for you by stepping out of the past and bringing this into the present of 2003. This chapter, as my life, has been a transforming work over time with God teaching me even deeper truths as I have walked through the struggles. Coming to the point of quiet endurance of my aloneness, I needed to learn another point along this journey. My struggle with loneliness had brought me to the point of acceptance; yet, I found that I kept my heart tightly guarded and locked away and I seemed to be unable to give love or feel joy. There with the gates locked tightly around my heart, I felt safe. Then after all these years of feeling alone, I met a man whom I was afraid I could care for if I let him in. That was a frightening thought. Could God now at this time in my life want to give me what I thought was my heart's desire-a human companion? Adding to my dilemma was the fact that he seemed to need a friend. Yet, I knew how vulnerable I have always been to the emotion of love. What purpose would it be to allow this man into my life? After all, I had learned to be so content alone. In fact, I was truly happy alone with God when I blocked my mind from even thinking about love. Could I risk being hurt again?

I wonder if I should step in and attempt to develop this friendship or let it pass. There is a great chance that he will leave soon and never return. Perhaps my care and concern for him is meant only for my becoming a prayer warrior for this man and that may be my only purpose in his life. After all, that was all he had asked for—prayer. That is ok; but wasn't I still at risk of allowing my emotions to get too involved and desiring more. So, one day he had gotten very bad news which left him distraught. So I decided to step forward, invited him to dinner and told him that God's plan was best—even if that seemed to be the opposite of what we think we want. I too realized I had to trust God as well for the same. As was the case, once more I confused my empathy and concern for what I believed to be love. I began to feel my heart weep because I did not understand why God would allow me to be in a place where I could be hurt once more by my own desire to be loved. I really want only God's plan in God's timing, laying aside my own human desires. Haven't I learned in whose arms I can trust? Listening to a love song the other day, being the romantic that I am, I realized in whom I place my trust. The song is by All 4 One and has the line "These arms won't let your heart break". Suddenly as though His voice so clearly reached out to me, I knew whose arms would not allow my heart to break. I am cradled and held constantly in the arms of Jesus, my true love and bridegroom. I then realized my heart, which had come to fear and shun feeling love, could be overflowing with love and never be afraid. My place is to keep my eyes focused on my true love which is Jesus and remain morally and spiritually right. If He chooses one day to provide me with an earthly companion, that is wonderful. If not, that too is wonderful. He will protect my heart and He allows my heart to open freely to show and feel love without fear. What a marvelous truth. I can truly love and give emotionally of myself and know that He, my heavenly Father, protects my heart and won't allow it to break.

Being a romantic, I have often found myself dreaming of my Prince Charming coming to rescue me from a cruel and painful situation. Now I realize my dream doesn't have to be squashed. For I know that I am His bride and one day my Prince will come to take me to Himself. Until that day, I will prepare myself and I will freely show His love through me.

Your case may be different, perhaps you are not alone. Yet, in the home you find that your loneliness is present with a house full of family and you wonder if it would be better alone. It is not necessary for you to be alone to find His presence. Knowing His promise that He is there, seek out a few moments to spend alone in His presence; however, brief the moment. When was the last time you reached out to hold Jesus and sing the old hymn, "My Jesus, I love thee, I know thou art mine." Only He can be the love to your broken heart when it is crying in despair. He will renew you and give you the strength you need. He is always there, just stop for a moment, sit still and feel the brush of His hand upon your face and know the depth of His love.

My Dearest Heavenly Father, Please touch the heart of anyone that might feel lonely or desperate right now. Give them the blessed assurance of your truth, your presence with them. Comfort them, as you always comfort me in those hours that I forget. Remove their pain and suffering as only you can Lord. Let your love shine in them and through them to a lonely world. Give me the strength to always follow you. Prepare my heart to accept thy will always and to remember the truth that you in your infinite wisdom and love always know what is best for me. Keep my eyes focused on your face, knowing that you truly are the one who protects my heart and will always hold my heart when I feel it is breaking. You it is who will gently take it in Your hands and mend it with Your great and magnificent love for me. You are the true Heart Surgeon. Fill me with Your love. It is your will only that I seek for my life. It is in the name of Jesus, my blessed Savior and true love that I pray, Amen

Therefore, Loneliness

The man I thought God had brought into my life left. Shortly thereafter, God commanded me to move to Florida to take the current job with Florida Cardiology, PA. Just before I left the man returned to Springfield; but I knew what God had commanded so I left for Florida. I cried the entire trip. Twice more while in Florida, I would think that God wanted to fulfill my desire here on earth with a human companion; but, both times my heart was broken. The first broke my heart. The second still swears his love but wanted me as a lover only and I could not be that and remain true to God so I walked away. Finally, after all the years of my life; I had learned the truth about loneliness. Again, let's look back to the existentialist view. They say that all humans live a life of loneliness feeling that no one really understands them completely which does carry a thread of truth. We are each made with a purpose in our very unique ways. We each have been born to glorify God. Our greatest place of joy and fulfillment is found in our communion with God. Sin is the breaking force that prevents us from having communion with God because He being perfect righteousness and justice could not look upon sin. For that reason, God had a plan to send His Son who was also perfect righteousness to take our sins upon Him and pay the penalty once and for all, forever. He stands then and offers to each and every one who would accept this gift the wondrous opportunity of fellowship with Him. The glimpse of truth that I said is from the existentialist view is true and valid when referring to anyone outside of the companionship of God. Remember it refers to loneliness is that feeling that there is no one who truly knows and understands everything about my innermost thoughts and hopes and dreams. The truth there is only one who knows you intimately and loves you unconditionally—that is God.

Psalm 139 expresses this well,

"¹O lord, thou hast searched me, and known me.

²Thou knowest my downsitting and mine uprising, thou understandest my thought afar off.

³Thou compassest my path and my lying down, and art acquainted with all my ways.

⁴For there is not a word in my tongue, but, lo, O LORD, thou knowest it altogether.

⁵Thou hast beset me behind and before, and laid thine hand upon me.

⁶Such knowledge is too wonderful for me; it is high, I cannot attain unto it.

⁷Whither shall I go from thy spirit? or whither shall I flee from thy presence?

⁸If I ascend up into heaven, thou art there: if I make my bed in hell, behold, thou art there.

⁹If I take the wings of the morning, and dwell in the uttermost parts of the sea;

¹⁰Even there shall thy hand lead me, and thy right hand shall hold me.

¹¹If I say, Surely the darkness shall cover me; even the night shall be light about me.

¹²Yea, the darkness hideth not from thee; but the night shineth as the day: the darkness and the light are both alike to thee.

¹³For thou hast possessed my reins: thou hast covered me in my mother's womb.

¹⁴I will praise thee; for I am fearfully and wonderfully made: marvellous are thy works; and that my soul knoweth right well.

¹⁵My substance was not hid from thee, when I was made in secret, and curiously wrought in the lowest parts of the earth.

¹⁶Thine eyes did see my substance, yet being unperfect; and in thy book all my members were written, which in continuance were fashioned, when as yet there was none of them.

¹⁷How precious also are thy thoughts unto me, O God! how great is the sum of them!

¹⁸If I should count them, they are more in number than the sand: when I awake, I am still with thee.

¹⁹Surely thou wilt slay the wicked, O God: depart from me therefore, ye bloody men.

²⁰For they speak against thee wickedly, and thine enemies take thy name in vain.

²¹Do not I hate them, O LORD, that hate thee? and am not I grieved with those that rise up against thee?

²²I hate them with perfect hatred: I count them mine enemies.

²³Search me, O God, and know my heart: try me, and know my thoughts:

²⁴And see if there be any wicked way in me, and lead me in the way everlasting.

I will proceed to quote myself as I break this down to very simple terms for you O Lord, you have searched every part of my being and you know me now—from before the foundations of this earth and to eternity you know everything about me. You have always known every time I would utterly fail and each time you would lift me up. You have known my thoughts even before I existed. You have surrounded my path of life and even surrounded me when I laid down my armor to quit. You are acquainted with all my idiosyncrasies, all that makes me uniquely me. There is not a word that I have spoken but what You knew even before I said it. You even know every word yet unuttered that will come from my tongue. You have besieged me, surrounded me. You know all my past, my present and my future. You have laid your hand upon me. How can I ever be able to comprehend this? Knowing everything there is to know about me; yet, you chose me and you loved me. Where could I run so far that Your spirit would not be with me? If I ascend unto heaven or climb to a high spiritual plateau, You are there. If I make for myself a bed of hell here on this earth, destroyed by sins curse; You are still there with me. If I soar above the mountaintops high with wings of eagles or live in the deepest darkest trials of life; you are there to lead me through every step of my life and to hold me safe from even my own self destruction.

So, one day; finally, I awoke and knew that my search for that one person who knew me completely was over. In fact, He had been there by my side for 50 years. He had loved me before I was ever born. I had been searching for some cheap replica of the real thing. I had what I was searching for and had not seen Him in His fullest Glory. Christ had always been there—the greatest love of my life. Why did it take so long for my eyes to be opened? I don't know. Yet, I do know that I have not had a single day of loneliness again since the eyes of my heart opened to this truth. I truly cherish my aloneness now with my true love at my side. Christ is my bridegroom for whom I will await His return with rejoicing.

We are born with that void that needs to be filled. We may think the void comes from not finding a human companion. We search to fill it with friends and events and work. Then we find we are not satisfied. We search to fill it with a spouse and then become frustrated as we find they cannot fulfill that empty spot deep within our soul. The only one who can do that is God. We were created to have this close intimate relationship with God. All other relationships can be an outpouring of that relationship with God; but we must see them for what they really are. They are not there to fulfill us or our needs. Only God can fill that gap. Only God is that missing piece. I had glimpses of that truth placed before me all along the way; but it did not become that strong force welling up in my spirit which drove away loneliness. I cannot tell you the steps in this process. I can only assure you that if you continue to seek and savor Christ, one day you will awaken and find that the darkness of loneliness is gone.

Releasing Those Whom We Love-Prelude

I had not been able to eat for two days and the grief overwhelmed me as I stood in the cemetery for my husband's burial. I felt faint as though all my life was draining from my body. So many thoughts were flying through my brain until they all seemed to be scrambled. I prayed for hope. Had it only been a few days since I had really released Pete into God's hands. By that I mean, I had prayed one more time that God heal Pete. I had watched Pete suffer so in a deep depression with what appeared to be an overwhelming sense of hopelessness. He had described to me that the pain he felt was greater than he could ever explain. So this time as I prayed, "God please will You heal him—I don't know what to do. If the only way for his pain to go away is for you to take him home and he for certain knows Christ as his Savior, then I let go. But if he does not know you, please Lord become my voice that he may find you." It was only two days later that he died on July 23, 1994. My whole life had been wrapped up in Pedro Barba. I had loved him no matter what the problems. After all those years, I still got butterflies as I saw him walking down the street like some teenager in love. For many years my purpose in life had been to try to bring him peace and joy. I had gently tried to show him Christ through my walk and testimony. Now he was gone and I had the task to pick up all the broken pieces and the shattered lives of my sons to go forward. My boys were just becoming teenagers and had already suffered so much. How was I going to help them through this tragedy? I didn't know how nor did I know what to say to comfort them.

I had buried my father in 1993 after a massive heart attack and my brother in 1987 following a tragic car accident. My heart had ached with their loss; but this time I felt so lost in the grief that I wondered how I would go on. I looked at my sons and knew I must for them. I also knew that they had a lot of their own inner struggles to deal with. That became evident at moments while I watched them go through their teen years. Amazingly, they were such grounded children that really they did well in school, they were well mannered, and never really got into trouble. Still, I knew they had a lot bottled up deep inside. I saw it in their faces at times. The same was true of my dear Melissa who had suffered through all this and even more because she was living away from me with her father in California. Then I was diagnosed with cancer. All three stood with faces of strength and care, so only they know what they felt and suffered at that time. I did not know how to help. The only thing I knew to do was to pray and to keep pointing them to the only Comforter I knew, Christ Jesus.

As is sometimes the case, when I began to write this chapter; I still could not face the real issues which lead me to this chapter. For that reason, I transposed those feelings onto a friend instead. The truth was I really wanted to take all the pains or sorrows that came into my children's lives so that they would not have to face it. I wanted to block all the trials from their path. I was overwhelmed with this desire when I wrote this chapter back in 2003. God used a friend to teach me what I needed to know for my children.

Releasing Those Whom We Love

*"Hearken unto this,...stand still and consider the
wondrous works of God" Job 37:14*

The other day a dear friend told me that he had cried all night. He began to tell me of the pain he felt and the frustration he was experiencing because of not being able to see his dreams fulfilled. His description of his pain reminded me of how many times I had felt the same devastating pain. My concern and empathy at that moment rose so high that I wished there was a way that I could reach out and make all his sorrows go away or that I had a magic wand that could give him all that he dreamed of. Instead I fell on my knees before God and pleaded that he lift the burdens from my friend. I asked that God remove his pain and give it to me. I asked that God would grant all of his dreams and pass his sorrow to me to carry for him. I was amazed at how sincere my desire was to carry his pain and release him from his sorrow. I initially thought that my desire was good. Surely, God was merely showing me how to love more like Christ loves. That day I carried a heavy burden in my heart, though my friend was not aware of my prayer or my desire to lift his burden. I continued to remain in prayer. Yet, the response that God gave me surprised me.

I thought of all that God had taught me through the pain of my own life and of the strength and faith that was now mine for having walked through the valleys. In that moment I wondered that if I interceded for his pain, would I interfere with his reaching Gods greatest blessing? I found that I then had to return before God and ask that God send my friend a host of angels to guide him through his sorrow. I was reminded that "*he shall give his angels charge over thee, to keep thee in all thy ways. They shall bear thee up in their hands, lest thou dash thy foot against a stone.*" Psalm 91:11-12. I knew that God honors prayers that include His scripture prayed back to Him. So I prayed this promise before God on behalf of my friend.

I knew that I was weak because I did not know what to pray for, so I prayed for God's will to be done. I knew that God loved my friend with such a perfect love that he would not allow any pain or sorrow that was not also a part of His perfect plan for him. I also knew that in the midst of any sorrow that God allowed He would walk with him to lift him up and protect him with a band of angels. God provides His Comforter, the Holy Spirit, to protect him in the midst of his sorrow. It was at that moment, that I knew that I did not know what to pray for or how best to intercede. I was reminded that "*Likewise the Spirit also helpeth our infirmities: for we know not what we should pray for as we ought: but the Spirit itself maketh intercession for us with groanings which cannot be uttered. And he that searcheth the hearts knoweth what is the mind of the Spirit, because he maketh intercession for the saints according to the will of God.*" *Romans 8: 26-27.*

In simple faith, I then stood before the almighty Sovereign God and asked that He intercede in my prayers and in His infinite wisdom to give His best to those I love; even when I don't understand the plan. He who knows my heart, knows that I would gladly carry their pain and would protect all those that I love: my friends, my children and my mother. But the truest love that I can demonstrate is releasing them into the arms of the wise and loving father who can love them more perfectly than I could even imagine in my frail and human understanding. Has He not already taught me of His marvelous Love and Wisdom, which would only allow the best for these His children. If I have learned to trust Him with my own life, shouldn't I more easily trust Him with those that I love?

How often as a mother had I wanted to protect my children from all pain. But I knew that if I held them too tightly, they would never learn how to walk. I wanted to cover them with my arms and protect them from all harm, but I knew that if I put them in a bubble of protection of my own making it would fail. I had failed my little girl by wanting to protect her. Instead I have learned that the only way to protect them is to release them so that God's protective arms would cover them. *"He shall cover thee with his feathers, and under his wings shall thou trust: his truth shall be thy shield and buckler." Psalms 91: 4.* He, the God of the Universe, is able to cover and protect my loved ones under his wings. Is that not so much more than I could ever offer them myself?

I must at those moments remind myself of His Promise. *"And we know that all things work together for good to them that love God, to them who are the called according to his purpose." Romans 8:28.* He did not say that all things are in themselves good or without pain, but rather that *"all things work together for good"*. Most of my life I have quoted this scripture. I have continued believing that the final truth was that God would so work the circumstances that the circumstances would become good in themselves. I failed to grasp the depth of this scripture until one day I read the following verse 29. A light bulb suddenly went off in my brain as I continued my reading of Romans 8. *"For whom he did foreknow, he also did predestinate to be conformed to the image of his Son" Romans 8:29.* All the things that happen within the life of a believer are ordained by God. He gently weaves each thread of sorrow, pain, joy, and hope together in order to complete a final portrait of Christ. The more we look like Christ, the more we are able to also love Christ. The more we love Christ, the more we seek and savor His presence. We can then begin to see our sorrows through His Sovereign eyes. We begin to understand the purpose in our suffering. As we understand this we become more filled with awe of His Glory and all that He did for us. As that happens we begin to be filled with His Joy, His Peace, His wisdom and His love. The circumstances themselves may or may not change, but how we view those circumstances does change. It is this transformation that allows us to grow so deeply in faith that the darts of the devil cannot penetrate us. We are then made able to sing forth with joy and peace in the midst of deep suffering, to the extent that the sorrow cannot penetrate our being.

"*He that spared not his own Son, but delivered him up for us all, how shall he not with him also freely give us all things?*" *Romans 8:32.* He **will** give us all things. "*Delight thyself also in the Lord; and he shall give thee the desires of thine heart.*" *Psalm 37:4.* He will provide all the desires of our hearts and give us all things, as He transforms us into the image of His Son. The miraculous part is when we delight ourselves in Him, our desires transform. His desires gradually take over our desires. What better desires to have than those of a Sovereign, Omnipotent, Omniscient God. For Christ knew how to delight Himself in the Father. As we become transformed into His image, we too know how to delight ourselves in the Lord; that this promise may be realized. II Corinthians 3: 17-18 "*¹⁷Now the Lord is that Spirit: and where the Spirit of the Lord is, there is liberty. ¹⁸But we all, with open face beholding as in a glass the glory of the Lord, are changed into the same image from glory to glory, even as by the Spirit of the Lord.*" God's goal and His promise to the believer is to transform the believer into the likeness of Christ. How can I, my children, my friend or any believer ever look like Christ without carrying a cross at some time in their life?

Certainly Paul the Apostle understood this principle. He knew that his former desires and dreams were rubbish compared to that which he had gained in Christ. This is certainly shown in Philippians 3: "*⁷But what things were gain to me, those I counted loss for Christ. ⁸Yea doubtless, and I count all things but loss for the excellency of the knowledge of Christ Jesus my Lord: for whom I have suffered the loss of all things, and do count them but dung, that I may win Christ, ⁹And be found in him, not having mine own righteousness, which is of the law, but that which is through the faith of Christ, the righteousness which is of God by faith: ¹⁰That I may know him, and the power of his resurrection, and the fellowship of his sufferings, being made conformable unto his death;*" This from a man who reports of his life in 2 Corinthians 11 as follows: "*in labours more abundant, in stripes above measure, in prisons more frequent, in deaths oft. ²⁴Of the Jews five times received I forty stripes save one. ²⁵Thrice was I beaten with rods, once was I stoned, thrice I suffered shipwreck, a night and a day I have been in the deep; ²⁶In journeyings often, in perils of waters, in perils of robbers, in perils by mine own countrymen, in perils by the heathen, in perils in the city, in perils in the wilderness, in perils in the sea, in perils among false brethren; ²⁷In weariness and painfulness, in watchings often, in hunger and thirst, in fastings often, in cold and nakedness. ²⁸Beside those things that are without, that which cometh upon me daily, the care of all the churches. ²⁹Who is weak, and I am not weak? who is offended, and I burn not? ³⁰If I must needs glory, I will glory of the things which concern mine infirmities.*"

If I want my loved ones to be truly protected and to receive all the best that God has to offer them, then I must be willing to trust God and to release them freely into His arms. I must step aside and quit trying to manipulate the circumstances. God will provide them with "*every good and perfect gift.*" For "*every good gift and every perfect gift is from above, and cometh down from the Father of lights, with whom is no variableness, neither shadow of turning.*" *James 1:17.* There is no gift that I might give to those I love to compare with what I know God will give them.

My task of true love is to lift them up before God in prayer and release them. This is truly the best that I can give. If I try to hold them in any way, I will fail to allow His best for them. As I let go and I let Him, they will truly receive His best. As I lift Him up before my loved ones, I release them into His arms of love. "*Who shall separate us from the love of Christ? Shall tribulation, or distress, or persecution, or famine, or nakedness, or peril, or sword?. Nay in all these things we are more than conquerors through him that loved us. For I am persuaded that neither death, nor life, nor angels, nor principalities, nor powers, nor things present, nor things to come, nor height, nor depth, nor any other creature shall be able to separate us from the love of God, which is in Christ Jesus our Lord.*" *Romans 8: 35-39.*

Dear Heavenly Father, As I stand before you, I release into your arms those whom I love that you might perfect your work in them. Take them forth into the world where you would have them go, even when that is far from me. I know that your loving arms will bring them to a place of perfect peace and joy. Thou art able to accomplish your work in them and bring them all perfect gifts and fulfill the desires of their heart. Let me stand firm as their prayer warrior by allowing the Holy Spirit to pray through me asking that which is best for them. Let me always be mindful to lift them up in prayer. Help me to understand when my understanding fails and help me to fulfill the purpose that you have for me in their lives. Let Thy words flow forth from my lips when I know not what to say. Let my voice ever lift you up before them that they might see your awesome grace. Let me always trust you with their lives as I have learned to trust you with my own. It is to you whom I give all my praise and to Your Son be glory forever. In Jesus name I pray. Amen.

Therefore, Releasing Those Whom We Love

As I now look at my children, I am amazed at all that God has done. They display in their lives the fullness of His Grace, His love, and His truth beyond anything that I could have ever hoped for. They live out their faith every day, displaying it to the rest of the world. God has woven their lives with the threads of His love. So here are the steps to learning to release your loved ones.

1. **Remind yourself of God's Sovereignty.** Isaiah 40: "*28 Hast thou not known? hast thou not heard, that the everlasting God, the LORD, the Creator of the ends of the earth, fainteth not, neither is weary? there is no searching of his understanding. 29 He giveth power to the faint; and to them that have no might he increaseth strength.*" (Isaiah 40: 28-29)

   "*In the beginning God created the heaven and the earth.*" (Genesis 1:1)

   All things were made by him; and without him was not anything made that was made." (John 1:3)

   "*Thou art worthy, O Lord, to receive glory and honour and power: for thou hast created all things, and for thy pleasure they are and were created.*" (Revelation 4:11)

"I form the light, and create darkness: I make peace, and create evil: I the Lord do all these things." (Isaiah 45:7)

". . . whatsoever is under the whole heaven is mine." (Job 41:11)

". . . for all the earth is mine." (Exodus 9:15)

"For every beast of the forest is mine, and the cattle upon a thousand hills." (Psalms 50:10)

". . . for the world is mine, and the fulness thereof." (Psalms 50:12)

2. **Remind yourself of His Omnipotence**

[27] For the LORD of hosts hath purposed, and who shall disannul it? and his hand is stretched out, and who shall turn it back? [28] In the year that king Ahaz died was this burden (Isaiah 14: 27-28)

[17] Ah Lord GOD! behold, thou hast made the heaven and the earth by thy great power and stretched out arm, and there is nothing too hard for thee: (Jeremiah 32: 17)

behold, one like the Son of man came with the clouds of heaven, and came to the Ancient of days, and they brought him near before him. [14] And there was given him dominion, and glory, and a kingdom, that all people, nations, and languages, should serve him: his dominion is an everlasting dominion, which shall not pass away, and his kingdom that which shall not be destroyed. (Daniel 7: 13-14)

For with God nothing shall be impossible (Luke1:37)

for I am God, and there is none else; I am God, and there is none like me, ¹⁰Declaring the end from the beginning, and from ancient times the things that are not yet done, saying, My counsel shall stand, and I will do all my pleasure (Isaiah 46:9-10)

3. Remind Yourself of God's Omniscience

⁴He telleth the number of the stars; he calleth them all by their names. ⁵Great is our Lord, and of great power: his understanding is infinite (Psalm 147: 4-5)

⁴He telleth the number of the stars; he calleth them all by their names. ⁵Great is our Lord, and of great power: his understanding is infinite (Job 37: 4-5)

³The eyes of the LORD are in every place, beholding the evil and the good (Proverbs 15: 3)

²⁹Are not two sparrows sold for a farthing? and one of them shall not fall on the ground without your Father. ³⁰But the very hairs of your head are all numbered (Matthew 10: 29-30)

¹³The LORD looketh from heaven; he beholdeth all the sons of men. ¹⁴From the place of his habitation he looketh upon all the inhabitants of the earth (Psalm 33: 13-14)

⁹And thou, Solomon my son, know thou the God of thy father, and serve him with a perfect heart and with a willing mind: for the LORD searcheth all hearts, and understandeth all the imaginations of the thoughts: if thou seek him, he will be found of thee; but if thou forsake him, he will cast thee off for ever. (I Chronicles 28:9)

4. Remind Yourself of God's Omnipresence

²⁴Can any hide himself in secret places that I shall not see him? saith the LORD. Do not fill heaven and earth? saith the LORD
(Jeremiah 23: 24)

¹⁹Go ye therefore, and teach all nations, baptizing them in the name of the Father, and of the Son, and of the Holy Ghost: ²⁰Teaching them to observe all things whatsoever I have commanded you: and, lo, I am with you always, even unto the end of the world. Amen
(Matthew 28:19-20)

¹⁶And I will pray the Father, and he shall give you another Comforter, that he may abide with you for ever; ¹⁷Even the Spirit of truth; whom the world cannot receive, because it seeth him not, neither knoweth him: but ye know him; for he dwelleth with you, and shall be in you. (John 14:15-17)

⁷Whither shall I go from thy spirit? or whither shall I flee from thy presence? ⁸If I ascend up into heaven, thou art there: if I make my bed in hell, behold, thou art there. ⁹If I take the wings of the morning, and dwell in the uttermost parts of the sea; ¹⁰Even there shall thy hand lead me, and thy right hand shall hold me. ¹¹If I say, Surely the darkness shall cover me; even the night shall be light about me. ¹²Yea, the darkness hideth not from thee; but the night shineth as the day: the darkness and the light are both alike to thee.
(Psalm 139: 7-12)

5. Remind Yourself of God's Love

¹⁶For God so loved the world, that he gave his only begotten Son, that whosoever believeth in him should not perish, but have everlasting life. ¹⁷For God sent not his Son into the world to condemn the *world; but that the world through him might be saved. ¹⁸He that believeth on him is not condemned: but he that believeth not is condemned already, because he hath not believed in the name of the only begotten Son of God. ¹⁹And this is the condemnation, that light is come into the world, and men loved darkness rather than light, because their deeds were evil.* (John 3: 16-19)

⁷How excellent is thy lovingkindness, O God! therefore the children of men put their trust under the shadow of thy wings. (Psalm 36: 7)

for God is love. ⁹In this was manifested the love of God toward us, because that God sent his only begotten Son into the world, that we might live through him. ¹⁰Herein is love, not that we loved God, but that he loved us, and sent his Son to be the propitiation for our sins. (I John 4: 8-10)

⁸But God commendeth his love toward us, in that, while we were yet sinners, Christ died for us. ⁹Much more then, being now justified by his blood, we shall be saved from wrath through him. (Romans 5: 8-9)

⁸The LORD is merciful and gracious, slow to anger, and plenteous in mercy. ⁹He will not always chide: neither will he keep his anger for ever. ¹⁰He hath not dealt with us after our sins; nor rewarded us according to our iniquities. ¹¹For as the heaven is high above the earth, so great is his mercy toward them that fear him. ¹²As far as the east is from the west, so far hath he removed our transgressions from us. ¹³Like as a father pitieth his children, so the LORD pitieth them that fear him. ¹⁴For he knoweth our frame; he remembereth that we are dust. ¹⁵As for man, his days are as grass: as a flower of the field, so he flourisheth. ¹⁶For the wind passeth over it, and it is gone; and the place thereof shall know it no more. ¹⁷But the mercy

of the LORD is from everlasting to everlasting upon them that fear him, and his righteousness unto children's children; (Psalm 103:8-17) In this fear really should be "stand in reverent awe of."

6. Remember that your departed loved ones who know Christ are standing in His presence- No more sorrow, no more pain, no suffering. Would I be so selfish as to deny them that blessing to hold them here on earth with me? Paul expresses this so well in 2 Corinthians:

¹For we know that if our earthly house of this tabernacle were dissolved, we have a building of God, an house not made with hands, eternal in the heavens. ²For in this we groan, earnestly desiring to be clothed upon with our house which is from heaven: ³If so be that being clothed we shall not be found naked. ⁴For we that are in this tabernacle do groan, being burdened: not for that we would be unclothed, but clothed upon, that mortality might be swallowed up of life. ⁵Now he that hath wrought us for the selfsame thing is God, who also hath given unto us the earnest of the Spirit. ⁶Therefore we are always confident, knowing that, whilst we are at home in the body, we are absent from the Lord: ⁷(For we walk by faith, not by sight:) ⁸We are confident, I say, and willing rather to be absent from the body, and to be present with the Lord. ⁹Wherefore we labour, that, whether present or absent, we may be accepted of him. ¹⁰For we must all appear before the judgment seat of Christ; that every one may receive the things done in his body, according to that he hath done, whether it be good or bad. ¹¹Knowing therefore the terror of the Lord, we persuade men; but we are made manifest unto God; and I trust also are made manifest in your consciences. ¹²For we commend not ourselves again unto you, but give you occasion to glory on our behalf, that ye may have somewhat to answer them which glory in appearance, and not in heart. ¹³For whether we be beside ourselves, it is to God: or whether we be sober, it is for your cause. [14]For the love of Christ constraineth us; because we thus judge, that if one died for all, then were all dead: [15]And that he died for all, that they which live should not henceforth live unto themselves, but unto him which died for them, and rose again.

In conclusion, whether it be that you are called to release a loved one to God in death or life; remember He who created the heavens and earth will accomplish His perfect work in them. So pray, always for each of your loved ones that God's will and purpose is carried out. Live a testimony of how God has worked everything together in your own life. Sometimes all you need to do is stand by quietly present while that loved one goes through whatever trial. Ask God for the wisdom to know when to speak and when to just stand firmly at their side.

Prelude for
The Potter and the Clay

In my adult life, I had moved so often because Pete would always be looking for a place where he felt he belonged and could excel. Due to his bipolar disorder, soon anyplace seemed the wrong place and so we would move. It did lead to a lot of adventure for a little country girl. I lived in so many places including Mexico. But in 2003, I was tired of moving and just wanted to settle down where I was for the rest of my life. All of the health issues had taken a toll on my physical health with each illness or surgery aging me rapidly. I was quite content in Springfield, MO; yet, God called me to move to Orlando. I really didn't believe Him at first. I had not been looking for a job; yet, as I was throwing away a nurse practitioner magazine-an ad caught my eye. Before I knew it, I had sent my resume and was asked to come for an interview. All my friends said not to go because I had to pay for all my travel and hotel expenses. Generally, that would not have been the case; but, I knew I was supposed to go for whatever reason God had. I was not certain that God had planned something in the course of the travel or if He had intended I take the job; but I knew I was suppose to go for that interview. After I interviewed with Florida Cardiology, PA and had met Dr. Sandeep Bajaj I knew I was suppose to take the job. This was even with a cut in salary. Fool? Maybe, but I knew God said go. I threw out one final fleece the last day I was there. I said God, if you want me to move to Orlando, let me find a place to live which is big enough for me and mom. The search seemed to be useless. The rental prices were way too high and I had almost given up when someone told to drive through a specific neighborhood near the office. Two hours before I would have to drive to the airport, I found a house that was perfect and the landlord was working in the yard at the time. Amazingly, they liked me and even held the house until I could move down, despite their losing 2 months of rent by waiting. So, God had spoken.

I knew that God's plan was better than mine; in spite of the fact that I was not certain what He had in mind. After all the years of financial struggle, suffering and poor health; I had learned that God has the right to do whatever He sees fit to perfect His work in me. There were many moments in which I moaned or wished for an easier road to walk; but, God knew what was best for me. It had always been His love that guided every detail of my life and there was no reason to doubt Him now. He had ever so gently molded this lump of clay and had been kneading out all the impurities in order to create a vessel He could use. Many times I did not see it as so gentle at the time; but, looking back, I could see His gentle hands molding me. He had been weaving and continues to weave a tapestry that will one day look like Jesus so as to reflect His own Glory back to Him. I later was led to write this poem which has been published as a song.

The Master Weaver

Broken threads my life you found
And with your love each piece you bound
A song of love your lips resound
With gentle hands, each thread you place
Oh could it be, amazing grace
A picture clear, my Savior's face
What joy divine, could it be true
Each broken thread, you only knew
When woven tight would look like you

The Scarlet threads my broken heart
The deepest sorrows blue impart
Each silver thread of tears that fell
You guide my life with such detail
A brilliant gold, your love divine
My sins were washed, a white sublime
You gently weave with skillful hand
The portrait mine that you have planned

Oh, let me Lord remember this
That I might know with joy and bliss
You did ordain my every tear
That I might learn to never fear
That I might trust the weaver's hand
And on this hope and promise stand
Your love will always know what's best
Your cradling arms are where I rest

Broken threads my life you found
And with your love each piece you bound
A song of love your lips resound
With gentle hands, each thread you place
Oh could it be, amazing grace
A picture clear, my Savior's face
What joy divine, could it be true
Each broken thread, you only knew
When woven tight would look like you

The Potter and the Clay

"cannot I do with you as this potter? Saith the Lord. Behold, as the clay is in the potter's hand, so are ye in mine hand." Jeremiah 18: 16

When I walk through pain, suffering, loneliness and deep valleys; I want to cry out to God and beg Him to change my circumstances. I have often questioned His reasoning and asked, "Why?" I have at times struggled within His hand wanting to go some other way; just like a small child who sees a shiny toy in the center of a busy highway wants to go after it and ignore the danger. Sometimes, I feel that He has walked away and is far from me; because for that moment I am looking at my own pain and cannot feel His love and joy; even though He is still present. I try to reason; "Surely, if He were present and truly loved me, He would do something to take away this pain." How can it be that my life is repeatedly filled with trials and sorrows if God is supreme? He knows the desires of my heart, why must my heart be broken over and over again?

Whenever we struggle to understand the why fore regarding all the trials that we face, God has provided us with an answer in the potter and the clay. This was the example God gave to Jeremiah. God's love for His people was so great; yet, they resisted Him and had turned away to worship other things. He sent forth Jeremiah to tell them of His mercy and His love for them that they might once more turn their faces to Him. It is in this setting that He sent Jeremiah to the potter's house to learn of His ways. *"The word which came to Jeremiah from the LORD, saying, ²Arise, and go down to the potter's house, and there I will cause thee to hear my words. ³Then I went down to the potter's house, and, behold, he wrought a work on the wheels. ⁴And the vessel that he made of clay was marred in the hand of the potter: so he made it again another vessel, as seemed good to the potter to make it. ⁵Then the word of the LORD came to me, saying, ⁶O house of Israel, cannot I do with you as this potter? saith the LORD. Behold, as the clay is in the potter's hand, so are ye in mine hand, O house of Israel.* *"Jeremiah 18:1-6.* We can also learn from the lesson of the potter.

In order for the potter to make a beautiful vessel from a lump of clay, he must first take the clay and knead it to remove any imperfections and air bubbles that may be present. Depending on the quality of the clay, this may be a difficult process of pounding and kneading. Once the clay is cleansed, he begins to work the clay gently in his hands to form it into a vessel of beauty. At times, the clay resists within his hands. He must pull, stretch and work the clay, sometimes gently and sometimes with great force so that it would yield into the form that he has meant it to be. It is necessary sometimes to break the vessel he has formed and reform it so that it can be perfectly and beautifully made. The more beautiful the vessel, the more work it takes to form. Without the work of the potter the lump of clay can never become a vessel of beauty and service.

This is also true of the Christian. We can never become a vessel of beauty or service without the workmanship of the master Potter. He knows all of who I am and what kind of vessel I could become in His hands. *"Before I formed thee in the belly I knew thee; and before thou camest forth out of the womb I sanctified thee." Jeremiah 1:5.* These words spoken to Jeremiah are the same for me. He knew me before I was ever formed in my mother's womb. He knew my heart, my strengths, my faults, and my weaknesses. He knew my every thought and my every need before I even existed. He knew exactly what would be needed to guide me to become the vessel that He created me to become. Despite that, He chose me and sanctified me to be His very own lump of clay. He knew exactly how much work would have to be done in order to create the vessel of service for which He had intended me. He knew what would be needed to bring me ever closer to Him and to transform my heart into one whose desires became conformed to His desires. He was prepared to continue this work unto His completion and then to bring me into the fullness of joy that He had meant for me to have-securely resting in His joy. He has patiently been stretching my capacity to love and to understand His Majesty. He has opened the eyes of my heart so as not to continue to view Him through these diseased human eyes. As we begin to see His majesty and Glory, we begin to understand His Sovereignty over every detail of our lives. Never growing weary of the task He always kept focus on what He had determined to be His Masterpiece of my life.

"And we know that all things work together for good to them that love God, to them who are the called according to his purpose. For whom he did foreknow, he also did predestinate to be conformed to the image of his Son, that he might be the first-born among many brethren. Moreover whom he did predestinate, them he also called: and whom he called, them he also justified: and whom he justified, them he also glorified." Romans 8:28-30. It is the knowledge of our Sovereign God that allows Him as the Master Potter to mold us from a simple, impure lump of clay into a vessel of light and love that can reflect His Glorious light back into this darkened world illuminating it with Him. He wants us to be vessels that shine forth mercy and love to a dying and destitute world. It is the greatest investment and achievement that we can have, leading the blind and the lost to Him. He also knows that our joy is dependent on our relationship to Him. He wants us to have joy, true joy which can only be found in Him.

Then, if I am to understand the pain and suffering that I face, I must first understand who God really is. I must be able to see His heart, His wisdom, and His Sovereignty in order to walk through the refining fires of my own life. It is only then that I can surrender myself into the Potter's hand and trust Him completely—no matter what my human eyes might perceive. Only by having an intimate knowledge of who God is are we able to *"lay aside every weight, and the sin which doth so easily beset us, and run with patience the race that is set before us, looking unto Jesus the author and the finisher of our faith." Hebrews 12: 1-2*

He has loved me with His perfect love. He proved this in the gift of His Son. *"He that spared not his own Son, but delivered him up for us all, how shall he not with him also freely give us all things?" Romans 8: 32. "For God so loved the World that He gave us His only begotten Son, that whosoever believeth in Him should not perish, but hath everlasting life." John 3:16.* He loved me so much that He endured the cross, the rejection, and the guilt, that I might have life. His love for me is perfect. For that reason, He will not allow anything in my life that is not wrapped in His love. He knew me and He loved me even before I existed. When I understand His heart of love toward me, I will accept any hardship that comes my way, knowing that His guiding hands of love have allowed it and is holding me, molding me through it. Whatever trial He has ordained in my life is ultimately to bring me closer to Him and thus to fulfill His purpose in my life which is also for my good.

Beyond His love is His wisdom, which is not limited by time or space. Before the world was ever formed, He knew me completely. *"But the very hairs of your head are all numbered." Matthew 10:30.* The number of hairs I have on my head changes constantly, as anyone knows when they brush their hair. This constantly changing feature is what He used to remind me that He knows each minuscule moment of my life as well as He knows the whole of my life. He knew every time that I would walk away, each time that I would doubt Him, and each time that I would fail. He loved me in all my frailty. His wisdom could see my entire life and know exactly what is needed to mold me into the vessel He would have me to be. There are no surprises for God. He never says, "Oops, I wouldn't have chosen her if I had known she would do that." He still chose this lump of clay and He knows what precisely what He is able to form in His hands from my life. Not only did He know me, He chose me. *"According as he hath chosen us in him before the foundation of the world, that we should be holy and without blame before him in love: having predestinated us unto the adoption of children by Jesus Christ to himself, according to the good pleasure of his will, to the praise of the glory of his grace, wherein he hath made us accepted in the beloved"* *Ephesians 1: 4-6.* He did foreknow me and thereby did predestinate me to be formed into the image of His Son. His great wisdom only allows those things in my life that are to work toward His glory and my joy.

He is also sovereign. *"In the beginning God created the heaven and the earth." Genesis 1:1* David knew of His Sovereignty, as he cried out, *"I will cry unto God most high; unto God that performeth all things for me." Psalm 57: 2.* God is He who has dominion over all things. *"And what is the exceeding greatness of his power to us-ward who believe, according to the working of his mighty power, which he wrought in Christ, when he raised him for the dead, and set him at his own right hand in the heavenly places, far above all principality, and power, and might, and dominion, and every name that is named not only in this world, but also in that which is to come: and hath put all things under his feet, and gave him to be the head over all things to the church, which is his body, the fullness of him that filleth all in all." Ephesians 1:19-23.* He it is who has power over the storm. *"And there arose a great storm of wind, and the waves beat into the ship, so that it was now full And he arose, and rebuked the wind, and said unto the sea, Peace, be still. And the wind ceased, and there was a great calm." Mark 4: 37-39.*

This same God of love, wisdom, and sovereignty is the Master Potter of my earthly vessel. If I understand fully who He is, how can I resist so when His hands reach out to mold me. Should we not all cry out as did Isaiah, *"But now, O Lord, thou art our father: we are the clay, and thou our potter; and we all are the work of they hand." Isaiah 64:8* He has sight beyond anything that I might see. He knows the plan that is **best** for me. Even when I don't understand the plan, He is in control. When it would seem that all around me is crashing in, I can rest assured in His promises. In the midst of the battles of life, I can claim the victory, for the victory is His.

That is the same as He will do for you. Perhaps today, the trials that you face seem too hard and you cannot understand what purpose they could have. Perhaps you feel that you are breaking into pieces that cannot be repaired. Just remember that you are in the loving Hands of the Master Potter, if you have ever accepted the gift of His salvation through Christ Jesus. He will always keep His promise to you and will form you into a vessel of joy and light. Cling to this promise. Steadfastly hold to this truth and He will show you His way. Always keep your eyes on Jesus, the author and the finisher of the race. He finishes it for us. He carries us through to the end and into eternity. It is He who accomplishes it. He alone will bring you peace and joy in the midst of your momentary sorrow.

Dearest Heavenly Father, Thank you for having chose me and for being in total control of the molding of my life. So often, I want or desire things in my life that may not be your plan for me. Thank you for seeing and knowing what plan is perfect for my life and overriding my shortsighted desires. It is you that I love and I just want to ask that when I glance to the right or left, help me to keep my eyes fixed on you. In the midst of the storms of life, guide me. Let me be able to always sing forth as Job "though He slay me, yet will I trust Him." As you help me to keep my eyes fixed on Jesus and on the promises of your word, I know that I will be ready to face the furnace of life and come forth as a vessel worthy of your light. Let me lay down myself daily before you and allow you to shine forth through my life. I know that I have peace and joy, no matter what is around me, as I rest in thy loving hands. It is in the name of your Son, my Savior that I pray. Amen.

Therefore, The Potter and the Clay

1. Always remember God's love for you.
2. God chose you
3. God wants the best for you
4. God knows what is best
5. God never makes a mistake.

What more can I say at this point than to remind you that each step of the way God is bringing you nearer to Himself and His glory. He has said in 2 Corinthians 3: *¹⁷Now the Lord is that Spirit: and where the Spirit of the Lord is, there is liberty. ¹⁸But we all, with open face beholding as in a glass the glory of the Lord, are changed into the same image from glory to glory, even as by the Spirit of the Lord.* As the Potter molds this clump of clay, I become changed into the glorious image of Christ. Little by little, glory by glory, bits of glory transforming me each step of the way. That is an amazing thought. Perhaps He chose me to walk so many tribulations that I might one day become a beautiful, exquisite piece of pottery that has just enough holes to spill out His glory shining forth through each hole and crack along my surface. Paul has said this in a far better way than I in 2 Corinthians 4:

¹Therefore seeing we have this ministry, as we have received mercy, we faint not;

²But have renounced the hidden things of dishonesty, not walking in

91

craftiness, nor handling the word of God deceitfully; but by manifestation of the truth commending ourselves to every man's conscience in the sight of God.

³But if our gospel be hid, it is hid to them that are lost:

⁴In whom the god of this world hath blinded the minds of them which believe not, lest the light of the glorious gospel of Christ, who is the image of God, should shine unto them.

⁵For we preach not ourselves, but Christ Jesus the Lord; and ourselves your servants for Jesus' sake.

⁶*For God, who commanded the light to shine out of darkness, hath shined in our hearts, to give the light of the knowledge of the glory of God in the face of Jesus Christ.*

⁷*But we have this treasure in earthen vessels, that the excellency of the power may be of God, and not of us.*

⁸We are troubled on every side, yet not distressed; we are perplexed, but not in despair;

⁹Persecuted, but not forsaken; cast down, but not destroyed;

¹⁰Always bearing about in the body the dying of the Lord Jesus, that the life also of Jesus might be made manifest in our body.

¹¹For we which live are always delivered unto death for Jesus' sake, that the life also of Jesus might be made manifest in our mortal flesh.

¹²So then death worketh in us, but life in you.

¹³We having the same spirit of faith, according as it is written, I believed, and therefore have I spoken; we also believe, and therefore speak;

¹⁴*Knowing that he which raised up the Lord Jesus shall raise up us also by Jesus, and shall present us with you.*

¹⁵*For all things are for your sakes, that the abundant grace might through the thanksgiving of many redound to the glory of God.*

¹⁶*For which cause we faint not; but though our outward man perish, yet the inward man is renewed day by day.*

¹⁷*For our light affliction, which is but for a moment, worketh for us a far more exceeding and eternal weight of glory;*

¹⁸*While we look not at the things which are seen, but at the things which are not seen: for the things which are seen are temporal; but the things which are not seen are eternal."*

Only God would choose fragile earthen vessels of clay to place within them" ***the light of the knowledge of the glory of God in the face of Jesus Christ".***

Prelude~True Joy

All the years of pain, sorrow, deaths, and financial disasters had begun to strip away the joy. I was becoming one of those somber Christians "bearing my cross until Christ comes". With all the suffering in my own life and in those of the patient's that I took care of; how could I display joy and still tell people about the seriousness of salvation? Yet, joy is not a giddy disregard for life. It is an expression of seeing the good and the hope in God's provision. Not patiently enduring, but rejoicing in His control over all.

Many Christians fail to understand that God is a joyous God. They walk about with somber faces and want all Christians to do the same. I was becoming one of those Christians who feared that if I were joyous, I would be disrespectful to God and to Jesus Christ who suffered so much for me. So, dutifully, somberly I continued on carrying my cross and believing that this was what a Christian does. Little did I understand how joy could be a part of the true Christian's life? Shackled by my own legalism I trod on stoically performing the work of the Lord and chastising myself for my imperfections. After all, wasn't that my duty?

How could I be joyous while enduring chronic pain? What kind of person remains joyous when lying in a hospital bed? Wouldn't joy make me appear a fool as I struggle to pay my bills and continue to work so many extra hours just to be able to make ends meet?

True Joy

"But let all those that put their trust in thee rejoice: let them ever shout for joy, because thou defendest them: let them also that love thy name be joyful in thee." Psalm 5:11

Throughout this book, I have revealed pains and sorrows. It has been filled with my doubts and fears, those things that would least allow any semblance of true joy. It has reflected many times on the truths of God that have brought deep peace or contentment in my life in the midst of deep trials and valleys. Yet, it has missed telling you of the depth of joy that one might find in that peace.

Perhaps, my error came in that I too believed that in a world of suffering, doubt and pain that it would be blasphemous to step beyond that point and reach for true joy in the midst of deep sorrow. It is amazing how God uses so many people plus His word to teach us what we need to know. He brings people in and out of our life at various times who bring the right message to our hearts if we are only open to receiving the message He has for us. Sometimes, your heart awakened in just the fashion to see a truth, never before realized in those who have spent a lifetime with you. When I least expected, I began to watch my children who taught me the reality of joy. Merely by watching their joyful approach to life I have learned from them without their knowing it. They seemed to always find a way to exuberate joy in the way they approached life and the way they could laugh. Particularly, Alberto has always refused to dwell on any pain or sorrow. Instead, he displays a spirit of joy wherever he goes. He lightens the lives off all who surround him by his spontaneous smile. Watching him reminded me of the person I use to be and that true faith was more than simply peacefully withstanding the torrents of rain, but rather it is ok to dance in the rain.

I had come to believe that the quiet peace, which carried me throughout my life to that point, was God's highest; but I learned differently. God is a smiling, joyous God. God promises us so much more and His truth can lead us to even a higher plane that truly allows us to soar.

*"The fruit of the Spirit is love, **joy,** peace, long-suffering, gentleness, goodness, faith, meekness, temperance: against such there is no law. Galatians 5:22-23.* This is a joy that exceeds all and allows one to sing out with joy.

He does not want us to just endure and carry our cross, but to throw off the pain and dance in His joy. *"Thou has turned for me my mourning into dancing: thou has put off my sackcloth, and girded me with gladness; to the end that my glory may sing praise to thee, and not be silent. O Lord my God, I will give thanks unto thee for ever." Psalm 30:11-12.* He means for us to step forth from our burdens and realize His joy that is greater than anything we have ever felt before. This is His gift to us. *"For I will turn their mourning into joy, and will comfort them, and make them rejoice from their sorrow." Jeremiah 31: 13.*

This joy is founded upon His promises and His gift to us. *"And not only so, but we also joy in God through our Lord Jesus Christ, by whom we have now received the atonement" Romans 5:11.* It is our position in Christ that brings us His joy and dancing. His song shall ever bring exceeding joy to our hearts. *"the righteous doth sing and rejoice." Proverbs 29:6*

Sometimes I fear that our lack of demonstrating this joy is that which prevents us from being true witnesses of our gift from God. Others in the churches past must have with their somber faces admonished those who want to demonstrate their joy. For that reason, James wrote *"Is any among you afflicted? Let him pray, Is any merry? Let him sing psalms."James 5:13.*

Surely, you think, this is impossible in the circumstances that you might find yourself. Yet, this is the case despite your circumstances, because the same God who has promised us His faith, His strength, His Joy. *"My brethren, count it all joy when ye fall into divers temptations: knowing this, that the trying of your faith worketh patience. But let patience have her perfect work, that ye may be perfect and entire, wanting nothing." James 1 2-4*

As with all of His gifts, they are not dependent upon our circumstances or who we are but are dependent on Jesus Christ and who He is. *"Now unto him that is able to keep; you from falling, and to present you faultless before the presence of his glory with exceeding joy." Jude 1:24.* We are partakers of this exceeding joy of Christ. He has not called us to merely endure our circumstances, but rather, to stand firm in His Joy. *"O send out thy light and thy truth let them lead me: Then will I go unto the altar of God, unto God my exceeding joy: yea upon the harp will I praise thee, O God my God." Psalm 43:4*

Let's look once more at this verse from Psalm and put it deeper into context. Chapter 43 of Psalm is the answer David found in his heart. The response God gave to him at a time that he had come before God with pain, fear and trembling. It is part and response to Chapter 42. David has come before God in deep sorrow, *"As the hart (deer) panteth after the water brooks, so panteth my soul after thee, O God. My soul thirsteth for God, for the living God: when shall I come and appear before God? My tears have been my meat day and night, while they continually say unto me, Where is thy God? When I remember these things, I pour out my soul in me for I had gone with multitude, I went with them to the house of God, with the voice of joy and praise, with a multitude that kept holyday. Why art thou cast down, O my soul? And why art thou disquieted in Me? Hope thou in God: for I shall yet praise him for the help of his countenance." Psalm 42 1-5.* In this case David teaches how to step forth from a simple claiming of the truth to reach the point in Psalm 43 of having found God's answer and having found exceeding joy. He was in deep despair and sorrow. Even having gone to the church and listening to others sing, he questioned why his pain and doubt persisted.

Yet, he sought out the true source of joy. He searched forth the waters and longed that he might have his thirst quenched. He cried out to the one he knew could fill the depths of his pain. He then sought out those who knew joy, to listen to their praise. He then claimed the truth and preached it to himself *"Hope thou in God: for I shall yet praise him."* He determined within himself that even if he at this moment could not feel the praise, he knew in whom he believed and that God would fulfill his joy. Not at this moment do I feel the praise or the joy, but I know that I will praise him and sing praises to him, because I know the Heart of God. From this step he made in recognizing that God would provide and that praise would come, he moved from mourning to **exceeding joy**. Not only did he claim the joy before it had arrived he asked that God be the provider of the light and the truth within his soul to bring about this praise. He claimed it knowing that God provided even the knowledge necessary for the joy. That God and God alone provides us with everything that we need to reach this point of exceeding joy in the midst of any circumstance.

It is He who can fill our lives with everything that we could possibly need. It is His joy that fills our hearts no matter what the storm. It is His truth that fills our mind and He is able to perform exceedingly beyond anything that we can imagine.

There is one more exceedingly important issue to discuss. Our joy is found in seeking and looking to the only source of true joy—God himself. So often we seek joy in things or desires of this world. We think that we might find joy in success, money, a house, a companion, good health, and yet, find that all these things are fleeting. Others seek joy by means of parties, drugs, or alcohol only to find that when the initial high is gone; they are lacking any joy. Man was made for pleasure in God's presence. Because we therefore seek pleasure; we often seek for it in things of this world and desires. Counterfeit joy is never sufficient to fill a man's spirit and that is why people who do not understand this constantly press forward to greater things; missing the only one who can fill man's heart with Joy. Only by taking your eyes off of yourself and the world's counterfeit joy can you find true joy in an intimate relationship with your heavenly Father who hears your every cry. He stands waiting to give you His joy abundantly, exuberantly.

Dear Heavenly Father, Thank you for always providing what we need and for having provided the gift of your Son and the Holy Spirit who intercedes for us. It is to you I sing this song of joyful praise. Thank you for those you have brought to me to teach me of your love and joy. Protect them and give unto them the desires of their hearts as they your servants have given freely of themselves. Let your words ring forth and provide joy to those who feel down trodden. Give thy exceeding joy to those who persist in carrying their crosses somberly in faith. Let them find that beyond their faith and trust is true joy beyond all measure. Thank you in the name of Jesus Amen

Therefore, True Joy

1. Look to Jesus the only source of true joy
2. Lay aside all those counterfeit hopes for joy
3. Seek the Lord with all your heart and soul
4. Read your Bible
5. Pray. Just talk to God all day long. I have found that quietly, in my head I can tell him about the things of my day while I continue to work. Apart from this take time in the morning and evening for quiet time with God. Perhaps, your time is limited. Do not let that prevent you from saying goodnight to your heavenly Father.
6. Remember that God is in Control, no matter what the circumstance
7. Like David, preach to yourself the truth. The world is talking how bad it is. The legalists are telling you that laughter is bad. Satan is whispering in your ear. Circumstances make you look at yourself. So preach to yourself louder than these other sounds, "I will yet praise Him. I will trust Him. I will rejoice in Him."